George Gillanders Findlay

The Books of the Prophets in Their Historical Succession

George Gillanders Findlay

The Books of the Prophets in Their Historical Succession

ISBN/EAN: 9783337037482

Printed in Europe, USA, Canada, Australia, Japan

Cover: Foto ©Lupo / pixelio.de

More available books at **www.hansebooks.com**

BOOKS FOR BIBLE STUDENTS

Edited by
ARTHUR E. GREGORY, D.D.
PRINCIPAL OF THE CHILDREN'S HOME AND ORPHANAGE
Author of "The Hymn-Book of the Modern Church," &c.

THE BOOKS OF THE PROPHETS

BY

GEORGE G. FINDLAY, D.D.

VOL. II

London
ROBERT CULLEY
2 CASTLE ST., CITY RD., AND 26 PATERNOSTER ROW, E.C.

OTHER WORKS BY THE SAME AUTHOR

THE BOOKS OF THE PROPHETS IN THEIR HISTORICAL SUCCESSION. Vol. I, To the Fall of Samaria. In the Series of *Books for Bible Students*. Third Thousand. 2s. 6d.

THE EPISTLES OF PAUL THE APOSTLE. In the Series of *Books for Bible Students*. Tenth Thousand. 2s. 6d.

CHRISTIAN DOCTRINE AND MORALS: the *Fernley Lecture for* 1894. Third Thousand. 3s.

"THE THINGS ABOVE": Ten Sermons, included in the 2nd Series of *Helps Heavenward*. 2s. 6d.

THE CHURCH OF CHRIST: Two Lectures delivered in Leeds. 1s.

The above are published by ROBERT CULLEY.

ALSO THE FOLLOWING COMMENTARIES

1 CORINTHIANS, in the *Expositor's Greek Testament*, Vol. II.

GALATIANS AND EPHESIANS: Two Volumes in the *Expositor's Bible*.

COLOSSIANS, in the *Pulpit Commentary*.

1 AND 2 THESSALONIANS, in the *Cambridge Bible for Schools*; also in the *Cambridge Greek Testament*.

THE BOOKS

OF

THE PROPHETS

IN THEIR HISTORICAL SUCCESSION

BY

GEORGE G. FINDLAY, D.D.

TUTOR IN N.T. LITERATURE AND CLASSICS,
HEADINGLEY COLLEGE

Vol. II
THE FIRST ISAIAH TO NAHUM

London
ROBERT CULLEY
2 CASTLE ST., CITY RD., AND 26 PATERNOSTER ROW, E.C.

"THE Bible becomes always more beautiful, the more one sees and understands how every word of it, while read in its widest application and in its personal bearing on oneself, carried a specific and direct message to the first hearers, determined by the given situation and the circumstances of time and place."

DOMENICO MORELLI.

PREFACE TO THE SECOND AND THIRD VOLUMES

AN apology is due for the late appearance of these volumes, which follow the first at an interval of eleven years. The long postponement has not been caused by idleness, nor by hesitation and misgiving on the writer's part; but partly by broken health, partly by the unforeseen interruptions of other work, and partly by the peculiar difficulties of the task and the continual appearance in the field it covers of fresh theories and suggestions, with which it was necessary to acquaint oneself. The delay, as I hope, has given some added maturity to this continuation of the work; it has so far swelled its size that two volumes are required to bring the story down to the Fall of Jerusalem and the close of Jeremiah's career. The fourth volume, on Prophecy in "The Exile and After," will be taken in hand speedily.

The standpoint assumed, and the method pursued, remain in general those that were adopted at the beginning and are stated in the Preface to Volume I. I cannot range myself as a partisan either of the "advanced" or the "traditional" school of Old Testament interpretation. I have endeavoured, by the aid of all lights available, in loyalty and candour to form my own conclusions on the vexed questions affecting prophecy, and to present those conclusions point by point in a clear, connected, and reasonable fashion. The purpose of the work, and its narrow limits of space, exclude many discussions on which one might have wished to enter, and judgements have to be stated for which the reasons are intimated rather than argued; but I have desired to assert nothing more positively than the evidence seems to warrant, contenting myself often with probability where a tone of decision would have been more agreeable, and seemingly more effective. The book has defects and omissions, of which the author is keenly conscious; other, and perhaps graver, faults will disclose themselves to expert eyes. It may at least afford him the opportunity of learning from those who may care to criticize his work.

The writer could wish that his labour may contribute something, within its own modest sphere, to the reconciliation of Tradition and Criticism, which must be brought about. Progress towards an understanding has been made of recent years. Some needless alarms have been dispelled, and some excesses chastened. The rights and duties of criticism (which is nothing more than instructed and reasoned judgement) in regard to Scripture are increasingly recognized—of the "higher criticism" occupied with the date, authorship, and composition of ancient documents, and of the "lower criticism" which examines the condition and traces the transmission of their text. It is now more generally understood that the old criticism (higher and lower) of rabbis and scribes and of pre-scientific editors and commentators, from which many of the views inculcated in the childhood of the older amongst us were derived, is bound to be amended under the new light which God has given to our times. The light is bewildering, and the process of readjustment is disquieting for the present. But let us possess our souls in patience; "the firm foundation of God standeth." More and more it becomes manifest that in its substance and tenor the Church's witness to the Bible is impregnable, and that the extreme and subversive opinions advanced in certain quarters are unhistorical and invalid.

The grounds on which we "think we have eternal life" in Christ's Scriptures and find them testify to Him, lie deep in their spiritual nature and their whole organic life. They are such as true criticism cannot impair; but which it may free from accretions and obscurities, helping us to reach a simpler, larger, and more consistent apprehension of God's dealings with mankind through Israel and through Jesus Christ. Such, at any rate, has been the writer's experience; and this experience is, he trusts, reflected in the chapters here presented.

My colleagues, Professor W. J. Moulton and the Rev. J. Hugh Michael, B.A., have given me valuable help in proof-revision.

GEORGE G. FINDLAY.

April, 1907.

CONTENTS

	PAGE
PREFACE	vii
CHRONOLOGICAL TABLE	xiv

THE ASSYRIAN-JUDÆAN AGE (*continued*)

CHAP.
XIII. THE JUDÆAN STATE IN ISAIAH'S TIME	1
XIV. THE EARLIER PROPHECIES OF ISAIAH: CHAPTERS 1–12	26
XV. ORACLES (CHIEFLY) AGAINST FOREIGN NATIONS: CHAPTERS 13–23	56
XVI. THE LATER PROPHECIES OF ISAIAH: CHAPTERS 28–33	97
XVII. THE MESSIANIC TEACHING OF ISAIAH	127
ANALYSIS OF ISAIAH, CHAPTERS 1–39	146
XVIII. THE REACTION UNDER MANASSEH	150
XIX. NAHUM, AND THE FALL OF NINEVEH	170

CHRONOLOGICAL TABLE

THE SARGONID DYNASTY AND AFTER.

THE SARGONID DYNASTY AND AFTER.[1]

ASSYRIA.	B.C.	JUDÆA.	B.C.	EGYPT, ETC.	B.C.
SARGON II accessit	722	Reign of HEZEKIAH 727 (or 714)–698 (or 685)		24TH EGYPTIAN DYNASTY till	708
Samaria captured; end of N. Israelite Kingdom	722	Career of Isaiah 740–c. 700		25TH DYNASTY (ETHIOPIAN)	708–660
Battle of Raphia	720	Prophecy of Isaiah 7 . 735		TIRHAKAH reigns	692–666
Capture of Ashdod	711	Prophecy of Micah 1 c. 724		Fall of Thebes (No-Amon)	664
Defeat of Merodach-baladan	710	Prophecy of Isaiah 20 . 711			
		Reign of MANASSEH 698 (or 685)–643		26TH DYNASTY, founded by Psammetichus I	c. 660
SENNACHERIB accessit	705			Rise of the Median Power	c. 650
Recapture of Babylon	704	Manasseh's visit to Babylon	c. 650		
War against Judæa and Egypt	701			Revolt of Egypt from Assyria	c. 650
Destruction of Babylon	690	AMON	643–641	Scythian devastation of S.W. Asia	c. 634–614
ESARHADDON accessit, after murder of Sennacherib by two elder sons	681	JOSIAH	641–608	Fall of PHRAORTES, Median King, in war with Assyria	c. 625
		Nahum prophesies	c. 635		
Rebuilding of Babylon	680–676	Assyrian yoke thrown off by Judah	c. 630		
		Zephaniah prophesies	c. 628		

Assyria.	B.C.	Judæa.	B.C.	Egypt, etc.	B.C.
Esarhaddon—*continued*.		Josiah—*continued*.		Cyaxares, conqueror of Nineveh, rules the Medes	c. 625–584
Capture of Zidon	679	Jeremiah's call	628		
Invasion of Egypt	670	Discovery of Law-book	621		
Asshurbanipal *accessit*	668	Deuteronomic Reformation	c. 620	Reign of Pharaoh-Necho	611–595
Destruction of Thebes	664	Battle of Megiddo	608		
Culmination of Assyrian power	c. 660	Jehoahaz	608	Nabopalassar founds Babylonian Empire, revolting from Assyria	c. 610
Revolt of Babylon	652	Jehoiakim	608–597		
Egypt rises against Assyrians	c. 650	Date of Jeremiah 26	608	Rule of Egypt over Syria	608–605
Destruction of Elam	645	Date of Jeremiah 36	605–604	Battle of Carchemish	605
First attack of the Medes	635	Habakkuk prophesies	c. 605		
		Rupture with Babylon	c. 600		
Asshuredililani *accessit*	626	Jehoiachin	597	Reign of Nebuchadrezzar	605–561
The Medes approach Nineveh	625	First Captivity of Judæans	597		
Scythians invade Media	625	Zedekiah	597–586	Pharaoh-Psammetichus II	595–589
Sinsharishkun (Saracos) *accessit*	620	Date of Jeremiah 28	593	Pharaoh-Hophra	589–569
		Ezekiel's first Vision	592	Siege of Tyre by Nebuchadrezzar	587–574
Fall of Nineveh; end of Assyrian Empire	607	Fall of Jerusalem	586	Invasion of Egypt	c. 570
		Death of Jeremiah	c. 580		

[1] The dates here set down are based on those of the Cambridge *Companion to the Bible*. Occasional variations from these may occur in the sequel.

THE BOOKS OF THE PROPHETS

5 THE ASSYRIAN-JUDÆAN AGE
(*continued*)

CHAPTER XIII

THE JUDÆAN STATE IN ISAIAH'S TIME

Isaiah a Statesman-Prophet—The Prosperous Reign of Uzziah—Reign of Jotham—Policy of Pekah—Invasion of Judah under Ahaz and its Effects—Advent of Tiglath-Pileser—Dominion of Assyria in the West—Conflicting Data for Hezekiah's Accession—Hezekiah between Assyria and Egypt—Drifting to Egypt—Rupture with Sennacherib—Shattered Condition of the Country—Hezekiah and Merodach-baladan—The Hezekian Reformation—Isaiah's Attitude to the Temple Cultus—Literature under King Hezekiah.

THE prophet Isaiah was contemporary with four (ch. 1 1), probably five, kings of Judah—Uzziah, Jotham, Ahaz, Hezekiah, and Manasseh. He lived and taught in Jerusalem, at the centre of affairs; he was versed in the politics of the day, and accustomed to stand before kings. The Rabbinical tradition that Isaiah was of royal blood is unsupported by direct evidence; but it accords with the attitude that he took toward Ahaz and Hezekiah, and with his passionate faith in Mount Zion and its ideal kingdom. The loftiness of his thought and the majestic accent of his style of themselves justify the title of the *royal* prophet which he bears. He played a leading part for forty years in the counsels of his country, and was the inspiring head of a vigorous and largely successful patriotic movement. Isaiah is indeed the last and greatest example of the *statesman-prophets* in Israel. His work, like that of Moses and of David, powerfully illustrates the theocratic character of Israel's national life, and shows how entirely state and church were one in the minds of men of the Old Covenant.[1] To understand Isaiah's mission and life-work, therefore, we must place ourselves at his standpoint and attempt to realise the situation of the Judæan monarchy and people in the latter half of the eighth century B.C., and the nature of the crisis—or rather the succession of crises—through which he was called to guide the nation.

[1] See on this point Ch. II of Vol. I on "The Calling of the Prophet."

Isaiah grew to manhood during the closing years of the long and prosperous reign of Uzziah (or Azariah, about 780-740 B.C.), "whose name spread far abroad, for he was marvellously helped till he became strong" (2 Chron. 26 15). The prophet's earliest discourses "concerning Judah and Jerusalem" (chs. 2-5), delivered soon after Uzziah's death (ch. 6), describe a people in much the same flourishing condition in which Amos had found the Samarian kingdom thirty years before.[1] Foreign trade is thriving, the "land is full of silver and gold" (ch. 2 7. 16); and the wealthy classes are swollen with pride and luxury (2 11. 12 3 16-24).

The fierce reproaches of Amos and Micah against the magistrates and nobility are repeated with no less sternness by Isaiah, himself probably a man of rank: "Jehovah will enter into judgement with the elders of His people and its princes, saying: It is you that have consumed the vineyard of Jehovah; the spoil of the poor is in your houses! What mean ye that ye crush My people, and grind the faces of the poor? saith the Lord Jehovah of hosts" (3 14. 15; also 5 8. 23). It surprises us that social injustice, so crying and widespread, should have prevailed under rulers commended in the sacred

[1] See pp. 127, 128, also 132-13 f Vol. I.

history, as Uzziah and Jotham undoubtedly are; but the fact is unmistakable. In its foreign policy and military administration, however, the Judæan Government had been successfully conducted by these two kings. The Edomites and Philistines were held in subjection, the militia was kept in good training; the border fortresses were well equipped; and Judah was once more a factor of importance in political affairs. Agriculture and commerce were both prosperous (2 16). But religion, the vital spring of public welfare, was deeply corrupted. While the national worship of the temple was pompously maintained and the royal house remained loyal to Jehovah, private idolatry was rife amongst all classes (2 6. 8. 20), and gross immoralities and outrages were practised without shame (2 8. 9 5 18-24). God's people were become "a people of unclean lips." (6 5). Underneath the material splendour and outward orthodoxy that distinguished the half-century of Uzziah's reign, a social dissolution had set in, portending heavy calamities in the near future. These calamities Isaiah was called to predict (ch. 6); it was his work to denounce, and so far as possible arrest, the apostasies which were preparing ruin for a heedless nation.

Uzziah, like his people, sinned by pride

against Jehovah; he was smitten with leprosy, and suspended from his royal function some time before his death (2 Chron. 26 16-23). Of the sixteen years credited to Jotham in the books of Kings and Chronicles, the larger part probably was occupied by his regency in the place of his leper father, leaving a period of six years or less (740-735 B.C.) for Jotham's independent rule. Of him it is said that "he did that which was right in the eyes of Jehovah, according to all that his father Uzziah had done" (2 Kings 15 34); in 2 Chron. 27 2 it is added, "And the people did yet corruptly." Two signal events befell in this short epoch: the commencement of Isaiah's ministry of judgement, "in the year that king Uzziah died" (6 1); and the formation of the league of the kings of Damascus and Samaria against Judah. A cloud was gathering on the political horizon, soon to break in storm upon the careless Judæans. To Pekah (*Peqach*)—"the worthless shepherd," as we believe, of Zech. 11 15-17 (see Vol. I, p. 207)—belongs the shame of having lighted again the flames of civil war between Northern and Southern Israel, after sixty years of peace. It is noticeable, however, that *Rezin* (*Retsin*) always precedes Pekah in the references made to their alliance; we gather from Isa. 9 11. 12[1] that the Israelites had themselves been attacked by the Aramæans of Damascus, before they united with them at the juncture of 735 when Rezin was awaiting the onset of Assyria. These facts tend in some measure to exculpate Northern Israel. Pekah had apparently been forced into league with Rezin, and Rezin compelled him in turn to attack Judah.[2] Damascus had for the time recovered her ascendency over Palestine; she was attempting to combine the neighbouring states under her leadership in resistance to the Assyrian invaders, who were already operating on the confines of Syria. Jotham, and Ahaz after him, stood out against this confederacy. The latter Judæan king, finding himself in peril, appeals to Tiglath-Pileser for help, proclaiming himself Assyria's vassal (2 Kings 16 7. 8). As this crisis was impending, in the year 735 or 734, King Jotham died.

Jotham's death, which took place in middle

---

[1] The critics are all of opinion that ch. 9 8-10 4 is out of place where it stands, and belongs to the same strain as ch. 5. Ewald, indeed, definitely inserts this section between vv. 25 and 26 of ch. 5. It is manifestly antecedent to the Aramæan-Israelite attack on Judah (see pp. 36, 61–63 below).

[2] Dr Whitehouse gives a somewhat different account of these proceedings, in the very useful "Introduction" to Isaiah 1–39 in the *Century Bible*, pp. 10, 11.

life, was a calamity for Judah. Just when a strong and experienced hand was most needed to guide the helm of state, it passed under the direction of Ahaz[1]—in Isaiah's estimate a thoroughly incompetent ruler. Ahaz was the child of a degenerate and luxurious age—a man without faith or courage, frivolous, wilful, heathenish in disposition (Isa. 3 12 7 1. 2; 2 Kings 16 7-20; 2 Chron. 28 16-27). "As for My people," says Jehovah in Isaiah, "boys are their oppressors, and women rule over them." Ahaz was but twenty years of age at his accession, and this is the best excuse to be made for him. The Aramæan-Israelite forces, which Jotham appears to have held at bay, now swept the Judæan troops before them; they laid siege to Jerusalem, and were bent on setting a certain "son of Tāb'êl" (Isa. 7 6)—probably an Aramæan viceroy proposed by Rezin—upon David's throne. To this occasion belong the oracles of Isa. 7 1-9.

Although the invasion of Rezin and Pekah lasted but a short time, its effect was disastrous.

[1] It is a curious circumstance that Ahaz's name appears on the Assyrian tablets as *Jeho-ahaz*—the name also of Jehu's son and successor on the throne of Samaria. The conjecture is that the Hebrew writers (or editors) struck out from this evil king's name the prefix *Jeho* (*Y'ho* = Yahweh) because of his apostasy.

The country was ravaged when at the bloom of its prosperity; the army was destroyed, and a multitude of prisoners carried off captive to the north (see 2 Chron. 28 5-15).[1] The remarkable story of the prophet Oded's successful appeal to the Samarian leaders to restore the Judæan prisoners, that is related by the Chronicler, confirms the probability previously inferred upon other grounds, that the attack made on Judah by Israel at this time was made under foreign dictation and was against the conscience of the Israelites. Damascus, it must be remembered, was the hereditary foe of Northern Israel. The scene of 2 Chron. 28 15 indicates a popular reaction in Samaria against the unnatural alliance with Rezin. The military strength and prestige of Jerusalem had, however, been shattered by the blow now received. The Philistines and Edomites, as one might expect, seized the opportunity to revolt, and the Judæan kingdom was again cut off from the western maritime plain and from the Red Sea; the port of Elath was permanently lost (2 Chron. 28 17-19, 2 Kings 16 6)[2]; the sources of Judah's

[1] The *numerical figures* given by the text of Chronicles in this instance, as in many others, are incredibly large; otherwise there is little reason to doubt the truth of the story.

[2] We follow the reading of the *margin* of the R.V. in this verse. "Edom" and "Aram" were easily confounded in

commercial revenue were closed against her. The Southern Kingdom never recovered from the injuries received by it under Ahaz's luckless rule.

While Rezin and Pekah were laying siege to Jerusalem, Tiglath-Pileser fell suddenly and with irresistible force upon their territories from the north.[1] The situation was transformed instantly. Damascus and Samaria became the besieged instead of the besiegers; their own lands, as Isaiah had foretold, suffered an invasion even more cruel and destructive than that which they had inflicted upon Judæa. Samaria was reduced to subjection, and Pekah killed in a domestic conspiracy, before the year 734 was out. Damascus, after a long siege, fell in the year 732, Rezin being also put to death by his captor. The Aramæan kingdom of Damascus, which had played so active and eventful a part for the last two centuries, was at an end; the whole of Syria and Palestine lay at the feet of the Assyrian conqueror, to whom Ahaz paid at Damascus his miserable homage (2 Kings 16 10). The Assyrian government was now established over the west-lands. From this time until its

Hebrew script. That the *Syrians* appropriated Elath, the port at the head of the Gulf of Akabah, is highly improbable.

[1] See the account of this campaign in Vol. I, pp. 235-237.

fall was approaching toward the end of the seventh century, the sway of Asshur extended unbroken, though disturbed by many rebellions, from Armenia to the Egyptian border and from the Persian Gulf to the Mediterranean. In the case of an outlying province like Judah, policy dictated the continuance of the native dynasty and of internal autonomy, while a heavy tribute was imposed and strict guarantees of loyalty were required; the subject kingdoms were jealously watched and, so far as possible, deprived of external power. Ahaz had made his country an Assyrian dependency, and the pledges given by him were renewed by Hezekiah. This is one reason for Isaiah's rooted hostility to the Egyptian coalition, towards which the latter monarch gravitated. Even after Sennacherib's repulse Jerusalem still remained tributary to Nineveh.

The year of Ahaz's death (and Hezekiah's accession), to which the short prophecy against Philistia in Isa. 14 28-32 is referred, is uncertain. Vv. 9 and 13 of 2 Kings 18 (the latter identical with Isa. 36 1) furnish two contradictory data for the chronology of Hezekiah's reign. In the former passage we are told that the investment of Samaria by Shalmaneser commenced " in the fourth year of King Hezekiah."

The fall of this city, which came about after a siege of two years' duration in 722 or 721 B.C., is one of the best-established dates in ancient history. The statement above quoted assigns, therefore, the commencement of Hezekiah's reign to 728-7, the very year in which, as the Assyrian annals tell us, Tiglath-Pileser III died, being succeeded by Shalmaneser IV. But in ver. 13 we read that " in the fourteenth year of King Hezekiah Sennacherib came up against Judah," to be defied from the walls of Jerusalem at Isaiah's dictation and to see his forces annihilated by a stroke from the hand of Jehovah. Now the monuments show beyond doubt that Sennacherib's invasion of Palestine fell in the year 701 ; indeed, this king only mounted the throne in 705 B.C., when his father Sargon died. By the latter reckoning, Hezekiah acceded in 714 —that is, thirteen years later than we gathered from the previous datum. An error has crept into one or other of the discordant Hebrew figures.[1] The date of ver. 9 appears, on various

[1] Some critics would reconcile this contradiction by supposing that Ahaz placed Hezekiah by his side in the year 727, so that they reigned conjointly for twelve years or more. If so, Hezekiah's share in his father's throne was but nominal during the period, since he must have been a little boy (allowing the correctness of the figures given in

accounts, the more probable; and the coincidence of the death of Ahaz with that of Tiglath-Pileser in the year 727 supplies, as we shall afterwards see, a clue to the enigmatical prophecy contained in the last five verses of Isa. 14.

In following the tangled course of politics through the twenty-nine years of Hezekiah's reign, we must bear in mind the cardinal fact that this king was from the beginning a declared vassal of Assyria. Throughout his reign, Egypt was incessantly meddling in Palestine, weaving her diplomatic webs and tempting the petty

---

2 Kings 18 2); and the case was quite different from that of Uzziah-Jotham. Dr Marti, in the elaborate article on "Old Testament Chronology" in the *Encycl. Biblica*, gives the years of Hezekiah's reign as 720–693 B.C. A further complication is involved in the figures given in 2 Kings 16 2 and 18 2 for the ages assigned to kings Ahaz and Hezekiah at their accession. If Ahaz was twenty when he came to the throne in 735, and Hezekiah his son twenty-five when he acceded in 727 (*ex hyp.*), then Hezekiah was born in his father's third year! Admitting the later date for Hezekiah's accession (714), Ahaz was a father at sixteen! Is it possible that, by a primitive error in the text, Hezekiah has been made Ahaz's son instead of his *brother*? The length assigned to Ahaz's reign in 2 Kings 18 2 raises yet another chronological difficulty. If he reigned "sixteen years," this king died in 719—a date according with neither of the inferences drawn from 2 Kings 18 9. 13. In fact, the figures of the Hebrew text for this period have fallen into inextricable confusion.

states that lay between her and Assyria by promises of support that she could never make good. Samaria fell a victim to the Egyptian lure in 722; and the Philistine city of Ashdod owed its destruction subsequently, in the year 711, to the same cause (see Isa. 20). Meanwhile, and during the early years of Hezekiah, the Judæan Government remained quiescent—partly, no doubt, through Isaiah's influence over the young king, partly in consequence of the defenceless condition in which Ahaz had left the country. It is possible that Jerusalem was *threatened*, more than once, by the Assyrians during the campaigns of Shalmaneser and Sargon,[1] in the years 725–720; several of Isaiah's Assyrian prophecies relate to this critical period. In 720 Sargon heavily defeated the Egyptians at Raphia[2] on their border; and this

[1] Sargon II succeeded Shalmaneser IV in the year 722, and before Samaria was captured. Sargon was the founder of a new dynasty (called by Maspero the *Sargonids*), which retained the throne to the end of the Assyrian empire.

[2] It has been contended that the "Musri" of the cuneiform inscriptions signified sometimes a North Arabian people of this name, quite distinct from the Egyptians; and this conjecture has led recent critics to assign to the North Arabian *Musri* much of what belongs to the Mizraim (*scil.* Egypt) of the Old Testament. Accordingly, the allies of the Philistines in the battle of Raphia are supposed to have been Arabians rather than Egyptians, but the probability

decisive conflict was followed by nine years of peace in the western provinces.

The battle of Raphia did not, however, cure Egypt of her passion for intrigue, nor wean the oppressed peoples of Palestine from their habit of leaning on this "broken reed." Hezekiah's prudent and careful rule had restored to the Judæan state much of its lost vigour. With renewed strength there came revived self-confidence and impatience of the Assyrian yoke, always made bitter to its subjects. An Egyptian party sprang up amongst the nobles of Jerusalem, which skilfully appealed to the national pride and religious faith, and which in the end gained the assent of the king despite Isaiah's strenuous opposition, and carried everything before it. *Drifting to Egypt* is the appropriate title under which Dr G. A. Smith, in his brilliant Commentary on the Book of Isaiah, describes the course of Judæan affairs from 720-705 B.C.

Hezekiah appears to have narrowly escaped being involved in the Philistine revolt, which resulted in the fall of Ashdod in 711. He took a leading part in the general rising of the west that ensued on the death of Sargon, in the year 705. About the year 710 the

still seems to lie the other way; and Dr Flinders Petrie, the Egyptologist, scouts the theory of an Arabian *Mizraim*.

25th dynasty assumed power in Egypt, and fresh vigour was infused into Egyptian policy. The new rulers were Ethiopians from the far south (see Isaiah 18, and comp. pp. 76 and 82–84). Their accession and warlike prowess evidently stirred new hopes of help against Assyria in the little kingdoms of Palestine. Although Jerusalem and its pious, but vacillating, king were delivered by miracle from the worst consequences of their revolt at this epoch and the Assyrian troops retreated leaving the city unviolated, the kingdom suffered a severe punishment and Hezekiah underwent deep humiliation (2 Kings 18 13-15): Lachish was captured and the border fortresses of Judæa dismantled; her territory was diminished, after it had been ravaged up to the walls of the capital (Isa. 30, 31); a multitude of captives were carried off (Sennacherib boasts of 200,000 on his monuments); and the fruit of nearly thirty years of patient and wise administration was swept away at a stroke. Only at the last moment, when the Assyrian despot had put himself in the wrong by his treacherous acceptance of Hezekiah's submission and when in his arrogance he had "reproached and blasphemed the Holy One of Israel," giving to the war the character of a struggle between himself and Jehovah, did the Almighty interpose to save the city—" for Mine own sake," He says, "and for My servant David's sake." Sennacherib had, however, already gained so substantial a success and won so rich a booty that, in spite of the loss of his army, he was able to pose as Hezekiah's conqueror on his return home. In this character he represents himself in his Annals and in the splendid bas-relief of the siege of Lachish exhumed at Kouyunyik, which is to be seen in the British Museum. He had subdued the whole of the Phœnician and Philistine coast, and defeated an Egyptian army, under Tirhakah (Isa. 37 9),[1] at Eltekeh near Ekron, reserving the capture of Jerusalem for the crowning exploit of the campaign.

[1] The mention of Tirhakah in this passage (= 2 Kings 19 9) raises a difficulty; for the monuments show that Tirhakah, who was the most notable Pharaoh of the Ethiopian line, only succeeded to Shabaku in 692—he reigned till *c.* 666 B.C. Some recent scholars, connecting with this fact the observation that *two distinct narratives* are combined in the account of the war with Sennacherib (Isa. 36 1–37 8 and 37 9-38: see "Isaiah" in Hastings' *Dictionary of the Bible*, ii. p. 492 *b*), have supposed that Jerusalem was *twice besieged* by Sennacherib, in 701 and (about) 691 B.C.—Tirhakah attempting his relief in the *second* siege—and that the two stories have been mistakenly blended by the author of 2 Kings 19. More probable is the explanation that Tirhakah led the Egyptian army against Sennacherib during the previous reign (so Flinders Petrie), or that Tirhakah's name has displaced in the Hebrew narrative that of his obscure predecessor.

Gloriously as the faith of Jehovah and the authority of His prophet were vindicated by the deliverance of Jerusalem, there was awful judgement mingled with this undeserved mercy. A mere "remnant" had "escaped of the house of Judah."

A scene of heart-breaking desolation and depopulation met the eyes of king and prophet when they looked out from the walls of Zion on the departure of the Assyrian foe. Hezekiah survived this disaster, and deliverance, only three years. He died in 698,[1] leaving his people in a condition even more prostrate than that from which he had raised them. In the next generation the work of Isaiah and Hezekiah was, to all appearance, completely undone. The reign of Manasseh, which covered the first half of the seventh century, was marked by a heathen reaction, the longest in duration and the most demoralising in effect amongst all the apostasies of Israel. This relapse sealed the doom of the Judæan kingdom, which was only postponed by the revival of religion under Josiah.

There were two events of capital importance occurring in Hezekiah's reign not yet referred to, in which Isaiah was greatly concerned—one of

[1] 685 B.C., according to the other calculation (see pp. 10-12 above).

them fully related, and the other strangely unnoticed in the Book of the prophet. *Hezekiah's sickness*, followed by the embassy from Merodach-baladan of Babylon, is described in Isa. 38 and 39. This narrative follows upon the Sennacherib story, and closes the account of Isaiah's public work. But the episode belongs to an earlier part of Hezekiah's reign, and not to its clouded termination, when he could have had no such treasures to show as those spoken of in ch. 39 ²; nor would Hezekiah's friendship, in his crippled condition, have been worth seeking by a distant enemy of Assyria. Merodach-baladan figures largely in the records of the Assyrian kings. He was their most crafty and persistent enemy. For over thirty years he maintained the combat with them; three times in succession he was conquered and driven out of Babylon, and still evaded capture and renewed the war. In 731 he first submitted to Tiglath-Pileser, and was deposed. In 721 he is reigning again at Babylon, and Sargon marches against him, claiming a victory; he held the Babylonian throne, however, until 710, when Sargon a second time attacks and now displaces him. No sooner is Sargon dead, than Merodach-baladan recovers possession of Babylon; and it is Sennacherib's first task to drive him out (704). Four or five years later the indomitable Chaldæan chief has once more raised his head; and it cost Sennacherib a hard struggle to inflict upon him the final defeat at the east of the Persian Gulf. There were two occasions in the career of Merodach-baladan when he might have sought the friendship of Hezekiah in the manner described: either in Sargon's time and about the year 712, when matters were ripening both in Babylon and Palestine for revolt against Assyria (Sargon accuses Judah, with other western principalities, of "speaking treason" just at this date); or under Sennacherib, in 704, at which epoch Merodach-baladan occupied the throne of Babylon for six months, and Hezekiah, then at the height of his power, was conspiring with the Egyptians and Philistines against Assyria. The embassy followed upon a severe sickness of Hezekiah, with which ch. 38 is occupied; and this sickness preceded the king's death by fifteen years (ver. 5) On the assumption, towards which we previously inclined, that Hezekiah reigned from 727 to 698 B.C., the occurrences of chs. 38, 39 fell in the years 713–712. On the other theory, that his reign extended from 714 to 685, the illness of Hezekiah and reception of the Babylonian envoys are carried down to a point thirteen years later, when Hezekiah had narrowly escaped destruction by Sennacherib, and Merodach-baladan was making his last desperate stand. This date does not commend itself. Those who refer the sickness and embassy to the time of Sennacherib's conflict with Babylon in 704, previous to his western campaign, must suppose some error in the "fifteen years" of Isa. 38 $_5$, upon either view of Hezekiah's term of kingship.

Of Hezekiah's *religious reformation* we have a brief account in 2 Kings 18 $_{3-6}$, largely amplified in 2 Chron. 29–31. Some recent scholars argue that this movement occurred at the close of Hezekiah's reign (on the assumption that he lived till 685 B.C.), and was due to the victory gained by Jehovism in the overthrow of Sennacherib, and to the effect of Isaiah's long-continued and powerful ministry. The absence in that prophet's writings of any reference to these reforms, and his strictures upon the temple service in Hezekiah's time (1 $_{11\text{-}14}$), are hard to understand on the assumption that the ritual had been newly rectified in the manner stated by the historical Books. In particular, Isaiah nowhere condemns the worship of the High Places, in ch. 19 $_{19}$ he appears even to regard with favour the use of sacred "pillars"—both of which customs Hezekiah is said to have abolished in 2 Kings 18 $_4$. On the other hand, the narrative of 2 Kings clearly places the reformation at the *beginning* of Hezekiah's course, and ascribes the success of his rule to this cause; and in Jer. 26 16-19 the revival under Hezekiah is attributed to the preaching of Micah the Morashtite, who, as it appears from chs. 1-3 of his Book,[1] prophesied the ruin of Jerusalem and preached against "the high places of Judah" before Samaria fell—*i.e.* at the commencement of Hezekiah's reign, in accordance with the succession of events in 2 Kings 18. Other considerations may be added that tell in favour of an early inception of Hezekiah's reforms : the effect of the fall of Samaria in rousing the Judæan conscience, and the reaction against heathenism and innovations in worship to which the disasters of Ahaz's reign naturally gave rise (comp. 2 Chron. 28 27).

Isaiah, after all, does not censure the lavish temple ceremony on its own account, nor as incorrect in itself, but because it was made a substitute for righteousness ; what he condemns is not disorder in worship, but hypocrisy in worship—the attempt to cover gross moral offences by zeal in religious formalities. Jeremiah's attitude to the reformation of Josiah a century later

---

[1] See Vol. I, pp. 246, 254-257. Tradition appears to have connected the reformation of Hezekiah with *Micah* rather than with Isaiah.

is quite similar. If, in Isaiah's final judgement, the restoration of worship effected by Hezekiah was a failure, we can understand the silence of his written prophecies upon the subject. The prophet may reasonably have wished to see a "pillar [or obelisk] to Jehovah" set up "at the border of the land of *Egypt*," without approving such monuments in his own country. And if Isaiah late in Hezekiah's reign still inveighs against Israel's "idols of silver and idols of gold" (31 7), it is likely enough that the destruction of these cherished objects had been neither so thorough nor so permanent as king and prophets desired to make it. On the whole, we see no good reason to set aside the statement of 2 Kings 18, that the reformation of worship was effected early in Hezekiah's reign ; and we presume, therefore, that Isaiah, despite his silence on the matter in his extant writings, took part in this movement, as his compeer Micah certainly did.

In estimating the condition of the Southern Kingdom in the latter half of the eighth century, attention should be drawn to the *literary culture* which distinguished Hezekiah's age. The writings of Isaiah, if we had no other witness, give evidence of the perfection to which the art of writing as well as of oratory had by this time been carried amongst the Hebrews. Amid the distractions of the times and the limitations attaching to the existence of a people so small and divided, the influence of spiritual religion had called forth in Israel since the days of Samuel a surprising mental development, of which prophecy and psalmody were characteristic products. With Isaiah and Hezekiah this progress culminated; and from the end of the eighth century we mark a decline of literary power and genius in the Old Testament writers, though the stream of their religious inspiration flowed on with undiminished purity. To Hezekiah alone amongst the successors of David and Solomon is any written work attributed. The thanksgiving psalm preserved in Isa. 38 10-20, the authenticity of which there is no decisive reason to deny, is the composition of a scholar rather than a poet. It is graceful, tender, and cultivated in style; it breathes a spirit of deep and submissive piety, and (if authentic) throws a welcome and pleasing light on the character of its royal author. This king's activity in other branches of letters is indicated by the collection of *Proverbs* traditionally assigned to him (Prov. 25-29): " These are the proverbs of Solomon, which the men of Hezekiah, King of Judah, copied out." Hezekiah seems to have employed a literary staff, whose business it was to collect and recopy older writings. Asshurbanipal, the great Assyrian king of the seventh century, did the same thing upon a larger scale. The research extended to a minor branch of literature like the Proverbs, embraced, we may suppose, the higher matters of law, history, and prophecy. Isa. 8 16 indicates the existence of a school or circle of devout students, who cherished the inspired writings, to whom this prophet commits his own teaching.

In all probability, we owe it to the religious care of Hezekiah and the contemporary Judæan prophets that the priceless treasures of North-Israelite literature did not perish with the dispersal of the Ten Tribes. Large materials from this quarter have been incorporated into the grand historical monument afterwards completed in the compilation of Genesis-2 Kings. The memoirs of Hosea, with those of Amos and Zech. 9-11 whose authors, though Judæans, ministered in Israel, had a terrible admonition for the generation of Hezekiah; Micah and Isaiah build on the foundation laid by these Israelite predecessors, and apply to Jerusalem with added force the reproofs addressed in vain to Samaria.

The events of Hezekiah's time gave birth to

a new outburst of sacred song, to which
Pss. 46-48, with others in the Psalter, are with
some confidence referred. And the reorganization
of the temple service, described (and possibly
idealized) in 2 Chron. 29-31, involved surely
the preparation of some primitive collection of
temple songs—a work in which Hezekiah's tastes,
if we may trust the indications of Isa. 38 10-20,
would lead him to take special interest. Thus
in various fields of the Old Testament literature
the hand of this pious and learned king has been
traced. At this epoch the constituent parts of
the Hebrew Bible began to take shape.

CHAPTER XIV

THE EARLIER PROPHECIES OF ISAIAH :
CHAPTERS I–XII

Unity of Isaiah 1-12—Want of Uniformity—Titles—The Great Arraignment—Chapters 2-5—The Exaltation of Zion—Traces of Ahaz's time—Chapters 5 and 9 8-10 4—Assyria in view—Isaiah and the Northern Kingdom—Chapters 6 1-9 7—The Coming Son of David—The Prophet's Call—Contents of Chapters 7, 8—The Child Immanuel—Symbolic Names—"God is with us"—The Church within the Nation—Light beyond the Darkness—Hatred of Foreign Alliances—Chapters 10 5-12 6—Assyria and Judæa c. 722 B.C.—Sargon leaves Jerusalem untouched—Israel's Messiah in contrast with the Assyrian Monarchy—Messianic Kingdom in Nature—Concluding Psalm (ch. 12).

THE first eleven chapters of the canonical "Isaiah" form a complete book by themselves, extending to about the length of the Book of Amos or Hosea, and covering probably some twenty years of prophetic activity. They are such a collection as Isaiah may have published in the early years of Hezekiah and not long after the fall of Samaria (722). There is in this volume a consecutiveness and unity of design, and a relevance in the structure and contents of the whole composition to the national situation in the years 740–720 B.C., which enable us to trace in it the arranging hand of the original author and to claim this as "the Book of Isaiah" in the strictest sense. This statement is made, however, with certain reservations. The compilers of the *Nebi'im*, who have combined with the later scattered leaves of Isaiah prophetical matter of a subsequent date, appear to have edited with some freedom even this earlier and finished book, which possibly did not reach their hands in a perfect condition. Along with his person, Isaiah's writings are likely to have suffered from the persecution of Manasseh. The critics detect displacements, interpolations, and additions to the genuine Isaiah even in chs. 1 to 12, on grounds the force of which in some instances is indisputable.[1]

[1] The seeming *displacement* of ch. 9 8–10 4 is pointed out on p. 6. For the probable *addition* of ch. 12—possibly even of ch. 11 10, and 11 11-16—see pp. 54, 55. The latter clause of 7 8 is reasonably suspected as a gloss (see p. 42); and the last verse of ch. 2, which is wanting in the Greek version, interrupts the connexion, and may be an annotation from some later pious hand. Such emendations as the above need

Hence, while the general plan and course of this book of prophecy can be clearly traced, its analysis in detail is far from easy. There is considerable inequality of style and treatment in it. In all probability the book has passed through several stages, and underwent modifications at the original author's hands; it is not evenly worked up and filled out in all parts. Chs. 7 and 8, in comparison with the rest of the work, read like notes and memoranda of prophetic conversations and addresses, and are full of obscurity due to their abrupt, elliptical manner; whereas the discourses of chs. 1 and 10 5-34 are specimens of finished Hebrew oratory; and ch. 3 16-24 supplies quite an elaborate inventory of the wardrobe of the fine ladies of Jerusalem.

The Title (1 1)—" concerning Judah and Jerusalem "—can scarcely have been intended in the first instance to cover more than chs. 1-12. Book II of Isaiah (chs. 13-27) brings us into

not disquiet us. It is a different matter when Hackmann (*Die Zukunfts-erwartung des Yesaia*, 1893), Duhm (*Yesaia*, in *Handkommentar zum alten Testament*, 1892), and Cheyne, in his later discussions (*Introduction to the Book of Isaiah*, 1895), proceed to excise such passages as chs. 9 2-7, 11 1-9, and deny to the original Isaiah the whole conception of the Messianic king, which has hitherto been regarded as the crown and glory of his teaching. The able critics referred to, in this attempt however overshoot the mark. On this subject, see Ch. XVII.

other regions and cities. Chaps. 2-5 are furnished with a title of their own, identical with 1 1 in range, but without any definition of time; the larger heading was doubtless framed to embrace the larger collection, within which chs. 2-5 were included. "In the days of Uzziah, Jotham," covers chs. 2-6; chs. 7-9 relate to the reign of "Ahaz"; and chs. 10-11 should probably be referred to "the days of Hezekiah."

1. Chap. 1, fitly entitled by Ewald "The Great Arraignment," forms a fine introduction to the book before us. It exhibits at the outset most of the features of Isaiah's mind and style—his elevation and breadth of view, the skilful disposition of his matter, his rich imagination and pictorial vividness and stately rhetoric, his powers of invective and appeal, his sternness and tenderness of soul, his awful sense of the majesty of Jehovah, his patriotism and loyalty to Zion. It reads as the report of an actual speech—the summary of many previous speeches—which serves by its comprehensiveness and full statement of the mind of Jehovah toward His people at this epoch to set the reader at the right point of view for understanding the pages that follow. A *preface* is usually the last thing in a historical work; its position is no index to the date of its matter. In view of

vv. 5-9, describing the land as desolated by a hostile force, this great discourse has often been referred to the invasion of Sennacherib in the year 701. But the sins charged on the nation in vv. 2-4, 10-17, 21-23, as the cause of its present sufferings, are those that form the subject of chs. 2-5 and of Micah 1-3; they belonged to the time of prosperity antecedent to the reign of Ahaz and the invasion of Judæa by the Aramæans (Syrians) and Israelites in 735; they could not fairly be ascribed in this sweeping way, to princes and people, in the period following Hezekiah's reformation. The denunciations of the prophet at the crisis of the war with Sennacherib run in a different vein (see chs. 30-33). At this time, moreover, Jerusalem is threatened but not actually invested—she is "as a besieged city"; and the invaders are vaguely described as "strangers," without the animus which Isaiah showed toward the Assyrians. On the whole, it seems likely that the Great Arraignment was delivered in an early period of Isaiah's ministry, when under the destructive attacks of her northern neighbours Judah was beginning to feel the troubles of the time, and when God was entering into judgement with a profane people, who had grown careless and corrupt during years of prosperity.

2. Chapters 2–5 contain "the word that Yesha'yah, son of 'Amoz, saw concerning Judah and Jerusalem"[1] before the crisis just mentioned. They form a well-digested *résumé* of his earliest teaching. Delitzsch entitles the section : "The Way of Judgement leading from Israel's false glory to the true." Dr Cheyne says :

> The burden of this prophecy is the necessity of a grand vindication of God's holiness, which will lead to a realization of Israel's destiny such as is at present impossible.

The idea on which it turns is contained in ver. 27 of the Preface : " Zion shall be redeemed with judgement." The Judæan kingdom is still flourishing and full of military pride (2 7. 15 3 2. 3 5 1) ; it has a navy[2] (2 16), as well as a numerous army ; foreign fashions are in vogue, feminine luxury

[1] The above title seems to indicate that the writing to which it belongs had a separate existence before its incorporation in Isa. 1–12, that, in fact, it was known by itself antecedently as "the word which Isaiah saw [here the LXX reads, by a slight variation in the Hebrew text, "which came to Isaiah"] concerning Judah and Jerusalem." This brief writing was circulated, we may conjecture, as a prophetic-political pamphlet in the reign of Ahaz. It became the nucleus of the whole Book of Isaiah.

[2] This must have been lost when Elath, at the head of the Gulf of Akaba, was wrested from Judah by the Edomites (2 Kings 16 6); see note on pp. 8, 9 above.

is at its height (2 6 3 16ff.); the rich are battening on the spoliation of the poor (5 7-9), as Amos witnessed it in Northern Israel a generation earlier (Amos 2 6-8 3 14f. 5 11f.) and Micah at this very time in rural Judæa (Mic. 2 1f. 3 1-4); drunkenness and sensuality prevail unabashed (3 9 5 11f. 22); idolatry and soothsaying are rife (2 6-9, 20). There is coming over the land and city "the blast of judgement and the blast of burning," like the sirocco-wind from the desert, which the Spirit of God will breathe in anger against His people (4 4). Jehovah will "arise" in "the glory of His majesty," "to shake mightily the earth";[1] He will bring down "the loftiness of man," that He may be "alone exalted" (2 11-21); He will "take away the whole stay of bread and the whole stay of water" (3 1); He will "lay waste His vineyard," bidding the clouds refuse to it their rain (5 6). The male population will be so reduced by war, that seven women will be dependent on a single man (4 1); the rich houses will stand empty, cornfields and vineyards will lie untilled (5 9f. 17). The gross irreligion of the day, the nation's insolent defiance of the Holy One of Israel, is, in Isaiah's view, the root of the evils existing and impending: "Jerusalem is

---

[1] The recent earthquake of Uzziah's time may have suggested this figure (see Amos 1 1 2 14-16 8 8; Zech. 14 5).

ruined, and Judah is fallen; because their tongue and their doings are against Jehovah, *to provoke the eyes of His glory*" (3 8).

Yet the awful visitation which the prophet foresees, is to be not for destruction, but for cleansing and renewal: "By the spirit of judgement and the spirit of burning" Jehovah "will wash away the filth of the daughters of Zion, and will purge the blood of Jerusalem from the midst thereof" (4 4). As the storm of His wrath subsides, the clouds and fire it has brought change their aspect and lose their destructive character; they supply shelter and light to the sanctified remnant left "among the living in Jerusalem"; they make a "pavilion" for her assemblies, serving the office which the pillar of cloud and fire rendered to Israel in the wilderness (4 3. 5f.). Thus Isaiah's first discourses end with the note of redemption, and translate threatening into promise. It is the note struck in ch. 2 2-4, a passage supplying the prelude of Isaiah's earliest teaching. The selfsame text we found quoted, in almost identical form, by his brother prophet Micah (Mic. 4 1-5); it was most probably an heirloom of prophecy handed down to both from a former generation (see Vol. I, p. 250). This faith in the destiny of Zion, so strong in Isaiah's breast and animating his whole life, had not sprung up in a day. The country prophet (Micah) holds it as firmly as the city prophet. It emerges in Obadiah and Joel (Ob. 21, Joel 3 20f.), who preached (if we are not mistaken)[1] a century earlier than Isaiah. By this time it had become the fixed idea of prophecy that Zion should be the centre of a world-wide, imperishable kingdom of Jehovah: "In that day the mountain of Jehovah's house shall be established at the head of the mountains ... and all nations shall flow unto it." It was Isaiah's work to make secure this rock of the hope of Israel, which stood fast through the storms of the coming age.

While the prophecies of chs. 2-4 were conceived and first delivered in the flourishing times of Jotham, at the outset of Isaiah's ministry, the allusions of 3 4, 12—to the rule of "children," etc.—suggest that it was written and published in its existing form when Ahaz came to the throne, at the age of twenty (2 Kings 16 2) and without even the wisdom of his years. In this connexion the reproach that "women rule over My people" (3 12), coupled with the denunciation of the "haughty daughters of Zion," which extends from 3 16 to 4 1, indicates feminine influence of

[1] See Vol. I, Chs. V, VI.

an evil kind as swaying the court of the young king. At the crisis brought about by the accession of the weak and childish Ahaz, Isaiah appears to have put in circulation this digest of his earlier preaching, with a view to avert the disaster which he saw impending over his country. Though chap. 2 2 (at any rate, 2 5)–4 6 is continuous in literary structure,[1] the phraseology of 3 16 ("*Moreover*, the Lord said," etc.) indicates that reminiscences of more than one spoken address were embodied in this writing. The topics we find in it had probably supplied the matter of many speeches delivered in the course of the years 740–734.

Chap. 5 is parallel to the foregoing and belongs to the same situation, but is quite differently composed. The prophet works up into a parable, under the form of a popular love-song, the figure of Jehovah's vineyard in 3 14. This song ends, by a tragic contrast to its beginning, in the denunciation of ver. 7, which becomes the starting-point of the six Woes pronounced upon the chief classes of Judæan sinners in vv. 8-24. The connexion of the last paragraph of the chapter, vv. 25-30, with the

---

[1] The last verse of ch. 2, as already signified, may be an interpolation. If original, it forms a parenthesis. The 'For' of 3 1 links itself to 2 21.

foregoing raises some difficulties. Ver. 25 closes with a striking refrain—"For all this His anger is not turned away, but His hand is stretched out still"—which we find taken up again in chs. 9 12. 17. 21 10 4, where it accompanies a prophecy of warning of a scope agreeing with that of ch. 5 and divides this into four nearly equal strophés. This later section of Isaiah (9 8–10 4) is unconnected with its immediate context, but is exactly in place when read continuously with chap. 5. It is generally agreed that 5 25-30 and 9 8–10 4 are of a piece with each other; the recombination appears to be best effected by inserting the latter passage between vv. 24 and 25 of ch. 5. Ver. 25 appears to be the fragment of a lost strophé, of similar length to the four of 9 8–10 4 preceding it, which applied to Judah or Jerusalem the strain of threatening already addressed in 9 8ff. to Samaria and Ephraim. The allusion of 9 12 ("Aram . . . devoured Israel") supplies an approximate date for this prophecy —viz. in the time previous to King Pekah's alliance with Rezin of Damascus, when the Aramæans were assailing Israel, in the attempt probably to force Samaria into their confederacy (see Ch. XIII, p. 6). Chs. 17 1-11 and 28, belonging to the same epoch (see pp. 61–63), should be read in connexion with this part of Isaiah's prophecies.

Through this whole deliverance (chs. 9 8–10 4 and 5 25-29) no word is said of Assyria by name, any more than in the Book of Amos; but its terrible shadow lies across the page. When Jehovah is about to "lift up a signal-flag to a nation from far" and to "hiss¹ for them to the end of the earth" (5 26), it is clear that a great foreign invasion is expected, which could only signify the coming of the Assyrian power, already threatening the whole West since the accession of Tiglath-Pileser III (see Vol. I, p. 218). By this datum the whole speech to which it belongs is thrown back to the reign of Jotham and the period antecedent to the Syro-Israelite alliance against Judah, and is thus associated in point of time with chs. 2–5, as it is in point of form with chap. 5 25.

In his grand oracle of judgement the prophet extends his survey beyond Judah and Jerusalem: "Jehovah hath sent a word into Jacob, and it hath lighted on Israel; and the whole people shall know it—*Ephraim and the inhabitants of Samaria*." Isaiah here steps outside of his usual province (9 8f.). Chap. 9 19-21 alludes to the recent civil wars in Northern Israel (about 737: see Vol. I, pp. 121–2). The prophet sees Jehovah

¹ The sound made by the *bee-keeper* to attract his charge; comp. 7 18.

"stretching out His hand" in "anger" and punishment over the whole land of Israel, for the crimes denounced were common to north and south. If the last strophé had been complete (represented now only by 5 25), we should probably have found Jehovah, at the end of this message, pouring on *Jerusalem* the heaviest vials of His wrath. Chapter 28, which is prefixed, out of chronological order, to the third section of the Isaianic prophecies, is parallel to the discourse before us. Accosting first the "drunkards of Ephraim" (vv. 1-13), it then turns to the "scornful men of Jerusalem" (vv. 14-22), who vainly imagine they have made themselves secure (by alliance with Assyria?[1] ver. 15) against the calamities coming on their northern kinsmen. The opening chapter of Micah follows the like course, pointing to the ruin of Samaria as a prelude to the fate of Jerusalem (see Vol. I, pp. 254 f.). The concluding passage of this prophecy of the great invasion (vv. 26-29) forms a

---

[1] So Robertson Smith in *The Prophets of Israel*, 1st ed., p. 284. Ewald, Delitzsch, and Driver prefer to think of a secret and crafty understanding with *Egypt*, such as the Foreign Office of Jerusalem arrived at in Hezekiah's time, and had frequently contemplated. On the other hand, Duhm and Kittel find this pact with Sheol in the use of necromancy and sacrifices to the infernal deities (see 8 19; 29 4?); compare, on this passage, pp. 102-104 below.

THE EARLIER PROPHECIES OF ISAIAH 39

most effective piece of word-painting; it depicts with marvellous vividness the wide-sweeping rush and terror of the Assyrian onset—the countless numbers, swift march, complete equipment, and destructive fury of the invaders, and the helpless misery of the invaded.

3. The third section of the First Book of Isaiah differs much, both in form and matter, from the foregoing. While chs. 2-5 are made up of a collection of warning orations, chs. 6-9 7 take the shape of *a biographical and historical memoir*, relating to a decisive epoch in the prophet's life-work and in the dealings of God with the Judæan king and people of his time. His encounter with Ahaz in the year 734 was the crisis of Isaiah's public ministry. From that time forward his prophetic authority was established, and his programme declared.[1] The advances made by this weak and traitorous young king to the Assyrian power, opposed by Isaiah, were the beginning of a train of calamities which would change the entire face of the nation's history.

Amid the throes of this struggle, with the

---

[1] About the same time Isaiah appears to have published the first written collection of his prophecies—the small volume of sermons comprised in chs. 2-5 (including 9 8-10 4; see p. 36 above).

ignoble Ahaz confronting him on the one side and the cruel and devastating Assyrian power advancing on the other, Isaiah was led by the Spirit of God to the sublime conception of the Messianic kingship associated with his name. In the brief and powerful strokes of ch. 9 c the prophet etches out the figure of that Divine "child" of the race and "son" of Israel, in whose person the universal monarchy of God's kingdom should one day be set up. From the prophet himself the record has come down to us of this supreme hour in his career and in the development of prophecy; no other but Isaiah could have furnished the graphic and intimate delineation of the conflict with Ahaz, the motives operating in it and the consequences issuing from it, that is contained in ch. 7. The reference to Isaiah in the *third person* occurring in 7 3 (otherwise the narrative runs consistently in the first person singular) indicates that the memoir has been worked over by another hand; from the same cause, possibly, it has suffered some abridgement, which would account for the obscurities that make ch. 7, and ch. 8 in a less degree, difficult to interpret (see especially 7 6. 9. 16. 19. 25). On the other hand, ch. 7 may have been composed of a series of memoranda or prophetic *notes*, that, for some unknown reason, the author had left in the rough. While Isaiah's fire and force of imagination are evident here, the lucidity and fulness of balanced expression by which his pen is commonly distinguished, are much to seek.

Chap. 6 stands out from its context, being an autobiographical introduction to the prophet's story of his encounter with the Judæan king. It shows how Isaiah had been prepared, and indeed compelled, to take this stand: he obeys the true King of Israel (ver. 5) in thus confronting the recreant son of David; it is his life's charge to vindicate the holiness of Jehovah at all costs against a rebellious and doomed nation. Jehovah has touched Isaiah's lips with cleansing and celestial fire, and has sent him to "this people" bearing a message that burns with His indignation. The crisis of 734 and his collision with Ahaz threw Isaiah back upon the sublime experience of six years ago, which gave him his personal knowledge of God and determined his prophetic vocation—an experience of the same order and the like momentous results with that which, eight centuries later, converted Saul of Tarsus into the minister of Jesus Christ.

Into chs. 7 and 8 oracles are condensed that were delivered on, at least, four separate occasions (see 7 3. 10 8 1. 5), though, probably, at no long intervals of time. (1) The first two of these were uttered to King Ahaz personally, when he was trembling, and his people with him, before the combined forces of Aram and Northern Israel, already threatening to capture Jerusalem and depose the son of David in favour of some creature of their own (7 1. 2. 6). The sentence of ver. 8*b* ("and within sixty-five years," etc.[1]) is probably a marginal gloss, an historical note attached to Isaiah's text by some later hand; for it interrupts the passage where it stands, and the information could have had no practical meaning for Ahaz, who is referred immediately afterwards (ver. 16) to a nearly approaching date for the fulfilment of God's word sent to him.

(2) In the case of the second conversation between Isaiah and Ahaz, the words addressed to the latter appear to extend from ver. 13 to ver. 17

[1] Ussher's explanation of this interjected statement is the most probable. He supposed it to refer to the plantation of Samaria with foreign colonists effected by the Assyrian king Esarhaddon about the year 670 B.C. This act of policy probably reduced the remaining Israelite population of the central districts to complete subjection, and had great significance for the foundation of the later Samaritan nationality. The historical note in all probability came from some editor like the author of the Book of Ezra, who was interested in the subject just mentioned, and who regarded Esarhaddon's action as completing the process of destruction for Samaria, the beginning of which is marked by Isa. 7 8.

only; the rest of the chapter, with its four short paragraphs each headed with the phrase "in that day," is made up of comments and after-thoughts of the prophet arising out of his expostulation with the king. The great "Immanu-el" sign given to the unbelieving Ahaz at once signifies the speedy overthrow of his two dreaded enemies, whose "land will be deserted" before the boy about to be conceived and receiving this grand name from the mouth of Jehovah "shall know how to refuse the evil and choose the good" (ver. 16), and conveys the assurance that *God is* still *with us* (His people and city) through all the ruin of the coming times and despite the unworthiness of king and nation.

The oracles delivered to the apostate king are followed up in ch. 8 by others; two distinct deliverances are traceable in vv. 1-4 and 5-10, while ch. 8 11–9 7 reviews the whole situation in a powerful discourse, which culminates in the great Messianic prediction of ch. 9 6. 7.

(3) The prophecy of 8 1-4 reinforces the oracles spoken to Ahaz. Some young bride, probably in the royal *entourage*, had been pointed out by the prophet a few months ago as destined soon to give birth to a boy who should bear the glorious appellation '*Immanuel*; now, the prophet himself is to be father of a son burdened with

the dreadful name *Máher-shalal-hásh-baz*, which describes the opposite aspect of the same imminent future, for it means *Speedeth-spoil—hasteth-looty*. This name of Isaiah's second expected son recalls the fact that, in his first encounter with Ahaz, he was directed to take with him his son *She'ar-yashūb*—i.e. *A-remnant-will-return*—whose name conveyed at once threatening and promise. Referring to these incidents and to the meaning of his own name (*Salvation-of-Jehovah*), Isaiah afterwards says, "Behold, I and the children whom God hath given me are for signs and for portents in Israel" (8 18; comp. Hos. 1 4-9, 2 1). Though the child is not even conceived, his name is publicly set down in writing before witnesses; and it is declared, "Before the boy shall have knowledge to cry, 'My father' and 'My mother,'[1] the riches of Damascus and the spoil of Samaria will be carried away before the king of *Assyria*" (8 4). At last the awful power, whose advent loomed dimly through the woes foretold in chs. 2–5 as earlier through the pages of Amos and Hosea, is distinctly named. "The king of Assyria" has,

---

[1] Comparing this note of time with that of the prediction given in 7 16, pointing to the same event, one infers that a considerable period intervened between the Immanu-el and Maher-shalal-hash-baz oracles,

in fact, been brought into the circle of Israelite politics through Ahaz's alliance with him against the kings of northern Palestine.

(4) The fourth oracle of this series (ch. 8 5-10) relates, in the first instance, to Israel rather than Judah: the two are distinguished in ver. 8; "the people" who "refuse the waters of Shiloah" (the temple-brook) "and rejoice in [1] Rezin and Remaliah's son" (Pekah), are surely the Northern Israelites referred to in ver. 4. They reject the gentle stream that "flows fast by the oracles of God"; they shall have in its place the raging Euphrates flood, which, after submerging them, will "sweep onward into Judah." Yet the name "Immanuel" is a safe watchword (it is repeated at the end of vv. 8 and 10); the horde of invading "peoples" of "far countries" is challenged to do its worst, for "God is with us"! The true Israel is imperishable (vv. 9. 10). Though the Assyrian flood will "reach to the neck," Zion shall yet lift her head above the waste of waters.

(5) The words of ver. 11, "Jehovah spake thus to me, with a strong [pressure of the] hand," introduce apparently a fifth deliverance of this period. The prophet turns from the unheeding king and

---

[1] Hitzig and Duhm, by a slight correction of the received Hebrew spelling, change "rejoice in" to "despair about," and thus apply ver. 5 to Ahaz and the Judæans.

people to address the band of "disciples" which has gathered round him, the nucleus of the church within the nation that hereafter becomes the hidden centre of Israel's religious life, and to "wait for Jehovah" who for the present "hides His face from Jacob" (vv. 16. 17). Jehovah seems to say of Judah, as once to Hosea (4 17), "Ephraim is joined to his idols: let him alone!" Isaiah will bide his time, standing with his children a silent token of God's displeasure and of the swiftly coming calamities (ver. 18). He knows well that "his word"—"the instruction [*torah*] and testimony" he now puts on record and gives in charge to his friends—will stand as the foundation of Israel's future, against the wizardry and necromancy by whose false lights the popular leaders are steering, on whom a night "without morning" is soon to fall (vv. 19. 20).

(6) Suddenly, while he is yet saying this, the night comes down upon the prophetic landscape, and Isaiah sees the Israelites in hunger and despair driven from home into the gloom of distant exile (8 21–9 1). But while he looks a new morning dawns out of the awful darkness for the land of the northern tribes—"a great light" shining where "the shadow of death" lay (9 1. 2). The diminished people is restored

in joyful increase (ver. 3, R.V.); by a bloodless warfare it is freed from oppression (vv. 4f.); the Messiah-king is born to it, who is invested with qualities and titles above human measure, and extends his peaceful, righteous, and enduring rule over the whole earth (vv. 6f.).

The condensed and obscure character of the last group of prophecies required a closer examination than was necessary for chs. 2–5; we shall return to the concluding verses of it in a subsequent chapter (XVII), on Isaiah's Messianic teaching. The political situation supplies the key to the prophet's utterances at this time. The vain fears and vain trust of king and people he traces to their radical unbelief in Jehovah and their rejection of His counsel (chs. 7, 8). The Assyrian alliance of Ahaz is as repugnant to Isaiah as were the later Egyptian intrigues of Hezekiah's court (chs. 30, 31). The storm he has seen approaching from the north [1] since "the year that King Uzziah died," is already breaking. The civil wars of the Samarian kingdom and of Ephraim against Judah are only a prelude to the all-destructive flood

---

[1] The Assyrian and Chaldæan invaders entered Palestine from the *north*, marching through Syria, and are therefore referred by the prophets to that quarter. The desert shielded the country from direct invasion on the eastern side.

that will soon pour from the Euphrates over the breadth of the land, sweeping away Damascus and Samaria alike, from which Jerusalem will barely emerge, as a great rock standing out of a drowned plain.

4. The third principal part of Isaiah's First Book is dedicated, and in part directly addressed, to *Assyria* (chap. 10 5–12 6): "Woe unto Asshur, the rod of Mine anger, in whose hand as a staff is Mine indignation"[1]; such is Isaiah's exordium. Asshur has executed Jehovah's sentence "against a profane nation" (North Israel, 10 6), and "Samaria" is now as "Damascus" (ver. 8); the Assyrians intend to deal out the same measure to "Jerusalem and her idols" (ver. 11). Samaria, then, has fallen; and this address cannot be dated earlier than the year 722. But its date is, in all likelihood, not much later. The overthrow of Jerusalem is the next prospective step in the conqueror's advance; and the taunting allusions put into his mouth by the prophet refer, beside Samaria, only to Aramæan

---

[1] Similarly in Jer. 51 20-21, Babylon is addressed by Jehovah as "My battle-axe and weapons of war," used to "break in pieces the nations"; but is told that, when she has served her turn in God's hand, He "will render unto Babylon . . . all the evil she has done in Zion"; and when Babylon falls the outcry is, "Now is the hammer of the whole earth cut asunder and broken!"

strongholds whose capture was antecedent to hers.[1] The irruption of ch. 10 28-38—whether the description of it be drawn from contemporary fact or (as seems more probable) from imagination—comes by the north road to Jerusalem, as though contemplated by the Assyrian host encamped on Samarian territory; not by way of Philistia and the west—the side from which Sennacherib in 701 assailed Judæa, and the usual line of approach for invading armies. Moreover, there is nothing said here about Egyptian affairs, which enter largely into Isaiah's preaching at the later Assyrian crises, from the year 720 onwards (see Isa. 20, and pp. 12-14 of Ch. XIII above).[2] The tone of chs. 10 and 11 is in other respects different from that of chs. 22 and 29-33, which relate to the war with Sennacherib. The prophet's language here is altogether that of comfort and hope for Zion (see vv. 24-27), suiting the early years of Hezekiah's reign, when the reform of religion set on foot by the young

[1] Carchemish fell under the Assyrians in 743; Calno, probably, in 740; Arpad in 739, and Hamath soon after it; Damascus in 732; Samaria in the same year, and finally in 722. On the policy and campaigns of Tiglath-Pileser, see Vol. I, pp. 231-237.

[2] "Egypt" is noticed in ver. 26, but only as supplying by the exodus a parallel for the coming redemption of Israel from Assyria.

king was in its freshness and the best results might be expected from it. The whole weight of the Divine wrath is directed against Asshur. Vv. 20. 21 point precisely to the recent policy of Ahaz and the exile of the Ten Tribes as the background of this address: "The remnant of Israel, and they that are escaped of the house of Jacob," are the Judæans and the fugitives from the north who had thrown in their lot with them; and when it is said, "They shall no more again *lean upon the smiter*," we are reminded of Ahaz's servility to Assyria, by which the spirit of prophecy had been deeply provoked a few years ago, and which is now a thing of the past.

The Book of Kings gives no hint of a collision between Judæa and the Assyrians at this early time; the danger passed over, and is unnoticed in that brief official record. But nothing is more likely than that disputes arose at this critical moment. It would be perfectly easy for Assyria to pick a quarrel with the little southern state, if she chose. During the long siege of Samaria the neighbouring Judæa must have suffered from military requisitions and plundering; and the southern tribesmen, whatever the royal policy was, could not withhold assistance from their distressed kinsfolk. Breaches of neutrality are sure to have occurred. Hezekiah was a man of opposite sympathies to his father, and presumably less complacent toward the suzerain power. Just at this time, too, the death of Shalmaneser IV and the change of dynasty at Nineveh (see Vol. I, pp. 219, 239) afforded an opportunity for renouncing allegiance, which the anti-Ninevite party in Jerusalem would turn to account.

The Assyrian troops, who have stormed and sacked Samaria, are on the point of marching south to seize Jerusalem, when this sublime defiance is uttered by the prophet Isaiah. The route is mapped out; the scouts are already moving in advance of the army (vv. 29-32), when the enemy's plans are suddenly abandoned and his forces called off, not improbably by tidings of revolt in some other quarter of the empire. Sargon seems to have accepted the apologies of Hezekiah, and contents himself with a diplomatic victory.[1] A second time Isaiah's inspired foresight is justified in the escape of Jerusalem from imminent capture—saved in the former instance *by* the Assyrians, when they attacked the Syro-Ephraimite coalition against Ahaz;

---

[1] The court of Jerusalem must have submitted—most likely it had never formally revolted—for Hezekiah continued to be a vassal of Assyria until Sennacherib's reign.

and now *from* the Assyrians, who were on the point of "doing unto Jerusalem" as they had the other day "done unto Samaria." This signal deliverance raised Isaiah's fame as a prophet to a high pitch; on the strength of it, we may conjecture, he published the enlarged Book of his Prophecies, incorporating in it the smaller volume issued in Ahaz's time (chs. 2-5). In chs. 1-11 Isaiah's entire prophetic work up to the year 721, or thereabouts, is put on record.

The relations of the Divine government to Assyria, the first of the military world-empires with which theocratic Israel came into contact since her redemption from Egypt, are defined in ch. 10; in this fact lies the specific importance of the oracle. Israelite prophecy takes on, from this moment, an imperial character. It begins to announce that "the kingdom of the world hath become the kingdom of our Lord and His anointed" (Rev. 11 15). The autocrat of the east who says, "By the strength of my hand I have done it, and by my wisdom," who takes "the riches of the peoples" into his hand as one "gathereth eggs" from their nests and "none moves the wing or opens the mouth, or dares to chirp" against him (vv. 12-14), little as he knows it, is a tool of the Almighty, an "axe" that the Holy One of Israel "lifts up" to "hew therewith," a "saw moved to and fro" by Jehovah's hand. Ere long He will shatter this instrument, since it "brags against" its Wielder (ver. 15). It is for Zion's sake and in the interests of God's kingdom in Israel that great armies march and convulsions shake the world, and that heathen empires rise and sink. The Assyrian shall not destroy Mount Zion, though everything short of this falls under his power. His yoke must be patiently borne till Jehovah's time for its departing (ver. 27).

Against the background thus furnished, viz. that of God's judgement on the character and fate of the Assyrian monarchy, the great Messianic picture of ch. 11 was developed. Just as the Prince of the Four Names, of ch. 9 6, shines in glorious contrast to Ahaz, the king of evil counsel and luckless war, so the rule of the coming "scion of the stock of Jesse" (11 1), by its peaceable and gracious character, presents an ideal in all its features the opposite to the Assyrian domination which, with brutal injustice and wild cruelty, is trampling out the weaker peoples. Vv. 1-5 describe the manifold wisdom, equity, and justice of the Messianic empire; vv. 6-9 represent its covenant of peace as embracing even the animal creation and restoring the amity of paradise.

The remainder of the chapter, consisting of two paragraphs of unequal length (ver. 10 and vv. 11-16)—each attached by the phrase "And in that day" (comp. 7 18. 20. 21. 23) to the foregoing prediction—extend the dominion of the ideal Son of David from God's "holy mountain" to the outlying regions whither Israel's sons have been banished, and from which they must be restored.

A doubt exists as to whether the second of these additions, or even both of them, are not a supplement to vv. 1-9 added by some inspired man of exilic times—a prophet taking up Isaiah's vein, but whose chief interest lay in the longed-for return of the Dispersion. Ver. 9, indeed, supplies a natural conclusion to the Messianic vision as at first conceived; but the references to the exiles are not a sufficient reason by themselves for denying the subsequent passages to Isaiah, who had witnessed with intense grief the deportation of the Northern Israelites (see 8 21-9 1). Moreover, the allusions of vv. 13f. point to the time of the divided kingdoms and of Israel's struggle for ascendency in Palestine. The note of ver. 16, with its figure of the "highway," is taken up again in ch. 19 23-25.

Chap. 12 we must, however, ascribe to some later poet. This hymn has devout beauty and sweetness of expression, but shows no touch of Isaiah's genius. It belongs to the softer strain of the post-exilic Psalms, whose phrases it repeatedly echoes (see the new marginal references of the Revised Bible). The addition of this appropriate concluding song at this point indicates that the several parts of the Book of Isaiah had come into the hands of the post-exilic scribes in detached form, and that chs. 1–11, up to their date, had existed as a distinct collection to be treated by itself.

CHAPTER XV

ORACLES (CHIEFLY) AGAINST FOREIGN NATIONS:
CHAPTERS XIII–XXIII

Contents of Isaiah 13–23—Position of Foreign Oracles—Form of the Fifteen Pieces—Against Samaria—"The Valley of Vision"—Jerusalem's Untimely Festivity—Date of Isaiah 17—A Personal Attack—Fragment against Asshur (14 $_{24\text{-}27}$)—Against the Nations (17 $_{12\text{-}14}$)—Against Philistia—Date of Isaiah 14 $_{28\text{-}32}$—Indirect Warning to Judæa—Tyre and Zidon—The Phœnicians in the Assyrian Wars—Conjecture as to 23 $_{15.\,16}$—Year of the Capture of Ashdod—A Biographical Extract—Against Moab—Edom (Dumah)—The Dedanites—Arabian Trade—Ethiopian Embassy—Date of chap. 18—Blessing for Egypt—Egypt and Asshur—Post-Isaianic Oracles—The Fall of Babylon—Date and Character of 21 $_{1\text{-}10}$—Great Doom-oracle against Babylon—Situation implied in 13 $_{2}$–14 $_{23}$—Theory of Divided Authorship—Chapters 24–27—A non-Isaianic Composition.

THE Second Book of Isaiah (chs. 13–23) is of a widely different complexion from the First. The prophecies of chs. 17 (mainly), 22 $_{1\text{-}14}$, and 22 $_{15\text{-}25}$ are concerned with home affairs;

but the rest of the volume is directed against the national enemies of Israel. Hence this collection is entitled *The Book of Oracles against the Foreign Nations*. The prophecies thus strung together differ greatly in style and literary form; they are not arranged in order of date, nor on any other discernible principle. The first and longest of this series, ch. 13 2-14 23, belongs, by every token of internal evidence, to the period of the Babylonian ascendency, and should therefore be assigned to some (unknown) seer of the Exile. The like conclusion is drawn, though not with the same confidence or general assent, in regard to the prophecy of the fall of Babylon in ch. 21 1-10. Chaps. 15, 16 we treated in Vol. I, pp. 116-120, as containing *an ancient oracle against Moab* revived and endorsed by Isaiah; a similar explanation may apply to the two brief and obscure prophecies preserved in ch. 21 11. 12 and 13-17. Isaiah's authorship of ch. 19 (against Egypt) and of ch. 23 (against Tyre) is much questioned; but the adverse reasons in these instances are not decisive. The last paragraph of chap. 23, however (vv. 15-18), concluding the book, appears to be a postscript added at the time of the return from exile (see pp. 74-75), and may afford a clue to the time of compilation. Zech. 1 5. 6, 14. 15, 19. 20 show that the returning

Judæans were students of older prophecy, and cherished strong resentment against their Gentile injurers of former times.

The epoch above mentioned supplies a suitable occasion for the collection of the scattered leaves of Isaiah found in this Book, which it would be natural, at that time, to preface with the great Woe upon Babylon (of chs. 13, 14) now just accomplished, since this Doom powerfully echoes the predictions of Isaiah respecting the kindred Assyrian tyranny. We cannot suppose, however, that a *contemporary* editor would have ascribed ch. 13 2–14 23 to "Isaiah the son of Amoz." This and other titles found in chs. 13–23 we may credit to the much later editor to whom the general form of Isaiah 1–39 is due. The structureless character of the Book and the lack of any traceable order of time or thought, in which it differs signally from chs. 1–12, compel us to recognize its post-Isaianic compilation. This volume appears to be a collection of the *disjecta membra prophetæ*, a heap of precious Isaianic "remains" put together with reverent care but with little sense of historical connexion, and enriched by one or more prophecies of a kindred stamp drawn from later sources.

A similar body of foreign oracles is found in the Books of Jeremiah and Ezekiel—in the latter case entirely authentic; in the former case, as in that of Isaiah, having apparently received extraneous additions. In the Hebrew text of Jeremiah this section of his prophecies closes the Book, being followed only by the historical appendix (ch. 52) corresponding to Isa. 36-39; but in the Greek edition (LXX) the Oracles against the Nations are interjected, at Jer. 25 13, into the middle of the chapters relating to Israel, and the same order appears in the original arrangement of the Book of Ezekiel, where the denunciations of the Gentile peoples interpose between the story of Jerusalem's fall and the vision of her restoration. To this latter analogy may be due the insertion of chs. 13-23 between chs. 1-11 and 28-33 of Isaiah,—both of which sections relate to "Judah and Jerusalem" and convey the main stream of Isaiah's teaching. Amos set the fashion of stringing together sentences of doom upon Gentile peoples, which he prefixed to his message against Israel herself; while the Book of Joel (still earlier, as we have supposed, Vol. I, pp. 95-116) concludes with a comforting deliverance of the like purport. Where a prophet had dealt with foreign peoples, it became the custom to collect separately his utterances on their destiny; such a compilation has here been made by Isaiah's successors. The prophecies against Assyria of chs. 10, 11, and 36 were not inserted here, since they had been already embodied in other collections. In the case of the three Israelite prophecies included in this volume, it is to be noticed that the first (ch. 17) is entitled "the burden of *Damascus*" and begins with a threatening against that city, although it bears mainly upon the fate of Northern Israel ; the enigmatical designation of ch. 22 probably obscured the fact that the oracles of vv. 1-14 and 15-25 relate to Jerusalem.

This Book contains fifteen distinct pieces—the longest of them covering forty-five, the shortest only two verses. Nine of these (eight in the LXX) bear the inscription *massa'*, "burden" or "oracle" (see Vol. I, pp. 58, 59)—"of Moab," "Damascus," etc.—which in some instances is presumably original, in others may have been supplied by the editor. Out of the remaining six, two (14 28 20 1) are dated "in the year that..." (comp. 6 1); two (17 12 18 1) begin, in succession, with the Isaianic exclamation *hoy*, "ah" or "woe" (comp. 1 4 5 8, etc.) ; the residue have no distinctive heading. It will be convenient to notice first (A) the three Israelite oracles; secondly (B), the foreign oracles of Isaiah himself, putting these as nearly as possible in order of time ; and thirdly (C), the post-Isaianic additions. Since the second, sixth, and fourteenth of the fifteen prophecies have no introduction of their own (see 14 24 17 12 22 15), it seems likely they were read as the conclusion in each case of the longer preceding oracle, so that the compiler reckoned the fifteen as twelve.

A.—Prophecies on Israelite Affairs

1. *Against the Kingdom of Samaria.*—Under the above head we must set down first "the burden of Damascus" (17 1-11), which already in ver. 3 associates "Ephraim" with "Damascus" and "Aram" in its threatenings, and thereafter dismisses the Aramæans from view. The title we may ascribe to some editor who derived it from the opening verses, disregarding the main scope of the prophecy.

This deliverance belongs to the early period of Isaiah's work, to the time when the Governments of Damascus and Samaria were allied (see pp. 5-6), falling in the year 735 or thereabouts. "Ephraim" has still his "fortress" and his "strong cities" (vv. 3. 9); "Jacob" boasts his "glory" and "fatness of flesh,"—the agricultural wealth of northern Palestine which was always an object of envy to Judæan eyes (comp. 28 1-4): the northern kingdom retains a large measure of prosperity and military strength, of which, in company with Damascus and Aram, it is soon to be miserably despoiled. The approaching calamity will resemble the reaping of a harvest amid thick "standing corn," or the shaking of the olives from a fruitful tree (vv. 5. 6). This warning can point to nothing else than the invasion of Tiglath-Pileser in 734-2 B.C. (see pp. 236, 237 of Vol. I), which resulted in the capture and political ruin of Damascus after a long siege, and the subjection of Samaria, deprived of its northern and eastern provinces, to the sway of Assyria. The punishment falling on Israel is attributed solely to her idolatry and neglect of "the God of her salvation" (vv. 8-12), much as by Hosea; and there is no hint of the complicity of Northern Israel in the Aramæan invasion of Judæa, which moved so strongly the indignation of Isaiah (see chs. 7 4-9, 8 3-6, 9 8-12).

The above oracle was therefore delivered after Pekah of Israel had come into alliance with Rezin of Damascus, but before the two declared war against Judah, and should accordingly be dated a few months earlier than that of chs. 7-9 (see pp. 6-7, 42). It is amongst the earliest extant of Isaiah's utterances, and supplies a link between the woes of Amos and Hosea pronounced on Northern Israel and those of Isaiah himself found in chs. 9 8–10 4 (see pp. 36, 37). The ruin anticipated for the Samarian kingdom is not so complete as that described later in chs. 9 and 10; "two or three berries" are still to be found "in the top of the uppermost bough," "four or five in the outmost branches of the shaken olive-tree" (ver. 6), while utter desolation is to overtake Damascus. In point of fact, the kingdom of Northern Israel, though sorely crippled, survived the invasion of Tiglath-Pileser for ten years.

2. *Against Festive Jerusalem.*—While ch. 17 counts amongst the earlier, ch. 22 with its "burden of the valley of vision" belongs to the latest of Isaiah's written prophecies, and is to be ranged with the series contained in chs. 29–33 and 36, 37. Between the two there lay an interval of more than thirty years. The *title* was suggested by the expression of ver. 5, "a day of perplexity, etc., from Jehovah of hosts in *the valley of vision*": the only plausible explanation is that which finds this spot in the Tyropœon hollow in the middle of Jerusalem (referred to in Zeph. 1 11 as *Maktesh*, "the mortar," also in Jer. 21 13), where Isaiah presumably resided, the mouth of which afforded the most assailable point in the defences of the city.

Jerusalem has broken out into wild and unholy mirth (vv. 1. 2, 13. 14) on occasion of the temporary raising of some dangerous siege, for which the city had found herself ill-prepared (5-11), when the circumstances called for "weeping and mourning" (4. 12). No one doubts Isaiah's authorship of this bitter denunciation, proceeding from a soul outraged by the frivolity of his beloved city. Sennacherib's siege, in the year 701, is the only occasion with which it can be connected; the allusion to "Elam" and "Qir" in ver. 6 shows that the enemy in view comes from the far east, and cannot be identified with the Israelite and Aramæan invaders of Ahaz's reign. The tone of the prophecy is, however, quite other than that of chs. 31–33 and 36, 37, relating to the siege of 701. This is a speech of rebuke and threatening; those breathe encouragement. The oracle is appropriate to the juncture in the war at which Sennacherib, after investing Jerusalem, drew off his troops (see 37 9ff.), and the populace broke into premature delight. On the resumption of the siege, when the king and people after protracted sufferings fell into despair and when the prophet had obtained from God a definite assurance of deliverance, he speaks in a different strain. Isaiah threatens Jerusalem in her presumption; he comforts her in despondency.

Verses 9-11 we understand, therefore, to point

ORACLES ON ISRAELITE AFFAIRS

to the first stage of the conflict with Sennacherib, when the city finds herself suddenly attacked with her preparations for the siege half complete; vv. 2b-7 may be taken to describe not a battle already lost, but the impending overthrow beheld in vision and set forth by the prophetic-perfect tense of vv. 2b and 3, which is depicted in gloomy contrast to the spectacle of mirth now witnessed in the infatuated city. Vv. 8-11 return to the ground of fact, setting forth the steps previously taken to put the city in a posture of defence, in which regard to God had been grievously wanting (ver. 11b). The apparent incongruity between this oracle and chs. 29-33, relating to the same crisis, may account for the fact that it is not found in that group of Isaianic prophecies.

3. *Against Shebna.*—Ch. 22 15-25 is a philippic directed against Hezekiah's prime minister—a notable instance of prophetic interference in political affairs. This is the only personal attack to be found in Isaiah; there are several such in the Book of Jeremiah. The Aramaic form of Shebna's name, and the absence of any reference to his father (contrast the case of Eliakim and "his father's house," vv. 20. 23), mark him out as a foreigner. This fact made his attempt to "hew out a" family "sepulchre on

high" amongst the princely houses of Judah and to "grave for himself a habitation in the rock" offensive to Isaiah's patriotism, and perhaps to his aristocratic feeling (see pp. 1-2). Beyond this act of presumption, no specific crime is ascribed to Shebna; but he is addressed as "thou shame of thy lord's house" (ver. 18), which implies unworthiness of character; and in nominating, through His prophet, Eliakim for the treasurership, by way of contrast Jehovah commends the latter as "My servant" (1s. 20), who "shall be a father to the inhabitants of Jerusalem and to the house of Judah" and shall bear "the key of David" (21. 22). One is tempted to think that Shebna was a promoter of the Egyptian alliance, which Isaiah had so strenuously opposed of recent years (see chs. 20, 30, 31), though nothing is here said to that effect. Vv. 24. 25 are, probably, to be read as a warning addressed to Eliakim in his turn, against *nepotism*: "Should they hang upon him all the glory of his father's house . . . every small vessel—the little cups, and the big flagons"—the weight will prove too great; "in that day shall the nail that was fastened in a sure place give way!" It was this very practice on the part of native officers of state, who were expected to find places for their whole clan, that led rulers frequently to employ strangers in the highest posts of government.

We find the names of both the rivals in the account given by 2 Kings 18 18. 26 (Isa. 36 3. 11) of the parley between Sennacherib's chief commander and the officers of Hezekiah at the walls of Jerusalem. Here Eliakim appears as " over the household," while Shebna is entitled " the scribe " or " secretary "; from which we gather that the foreigner had been deposed from the premiership in favour of Eliakim, but remained in high office, Isaiah's sentence upon him of exile and death (22 17. 18) being as yet unfulfilled. Shebna's abilities and experience, probably, made his services of value to Hezekiah. It is evident that Isaiah's influence over the king was not unlimited, and his dictation in matters of state may have been resented. The prophecy of Shebna's deposition stands quite detached, without a word to show its connexion with the events of the time or the course of Isaiah's ministry. We can only suppose that the eminence of the two statesmen concerned, and perhaps the signal fulfilment at some later date of the doom pronounced upon Shebna, led to the record and preservation of this remarkable address.

B.—Isaianic Oracles upon Gentile Peoples

4. *Against Asshur*, chap. 14 24-27.—This paragraph is in the vein of ch. 10, so much so that Cheyne and others suppose that it has by accident slipped out of its place, and should be restored to the great denunciation of the Assyrian, coming in most suitably between vv. 15 and 16 of ch. 10. Ewald preferred to attach it to the end of ch. 18. In any case, this is a characteristic Isaianic fragment, to be ranked with the grand orations of judgement upon Assyria, in ch. 10 5-34 and in chs. 33, 36 and 37. The compiler seems to have thought the passage *à propos* of the "burden of Babylon" preceding it in chs. 13, 14.

5. *Against the Nations*, chap. 17 12-14.—With the foregoing we associate a morsel in Isaiah's loftiest descriptive style, which stands unconnected with its context in chs. 17, 18, and has little to mark its date. Some, indeed, refer the passage to the Aramæan-Ephraimite invasion of Judah, and so make out for it a connexion with the foregoing prophecy of ch. 17 1-11; but it is *a sea* of peoples that Isaiah gazes upon as they pour over the defenceless land, and his language most fitly applies to the Assyrian armies, which were recruited from the peoples of a vast empire.

More feasible is the attachment of the three

verses to the next chapter. They would serve thus as a prelude to the Oracle for the Ethiopians, explaining the subsequent allusions of 18 4-6 and assuring the distant dwellers by the Nile that they need have no fear of the Assyrian onset, since its force will be utterly broken in Jehovah's own land. But the "Cush" prophecy of chap. 18 must be referred, as we shall see (p. 83), to the time of *Sargon*, when Judah remained in peaceful subjection to the rule of Asshur and its land had no reason to fear " spoilers " and " robbers " from that quarter. And if 17 12-14 were intended to form part of ch. 18, the paragraph should have been incorporated with it and made to follow, instead of preceding, the opening address to the Cushites. The invasion of Sennacherib, when the full tide of Assyrian conquest set in against the little kingdom of Judah, to be thrown back as if by miracle, affords the fittest occasion for this brief pæan, which is then seen to resemble ch. 30 27-33 and 37 21-35. But Isaiah foresaw the destruction of the Assyrian tyranny from a great distance, and there seems to be nothing which really forbids his having launched this oracle at a date coincident with that of ch. 9 4, or of 10 24-27 and 14 24-27.

6. *Against Philistia*, chap. 14 28-32.—A dated prophecy, like those of chs. 6 and 20 : " In the

year that king Ahaz died was this burden," *i.e.* according to our chronology (Vol. I, p. 122), in the year 727.[1] The Philistines are warned that though "the rod of" their "smiter is broken," their tribulations are only beginning, for "out of the snake's root a viper-brood will issue and its fruit will prove a flying fire-serpent" (ver. 29). The coming invaders of the Philistine cities will be worse than those from whom they previously suffered. The new enemy is descried, in ver. 31, as "a smoke *out of the north*," and is none other than the Assyrian conqueror (see p. 47, and Vol. I, pp. 229-230), who in fact overran Palestine repeatedly in the years following 727, and made the coast cities of Philistia, commanding the highway to Egypt, his first objective (Vol. I, p. 236). This district was, in fact, the key to the military occupation of Palestine. The Philistines had everything to fear from Assyrian ambition; they shared in every rebellion, and bore the brunt of each invasion in turn. This warlike little nationality appears to have perished in the course of the struggles between the Eastern Empires and Egypt, during this and the following centuries. "The messengers of the nation"

---

[1] The chronological reference is surely original. It is in the style of ch. 6 1 and 20 1. No one suggests a likely motive for the insertion of this particular date by a later hand.

(32) were doubtless ambassadors sent by the Philistine cities to the new king Hezekiah, seeking to draw him into league with them against Assyria (comp. pp. 12-14).

Since the threatening of ver. 31 repeats that of 29, the "viper" and "dragon" of the latter passage must be, like the "smoke out of the north" in the former, of Assyrian birth; and the "smiter" with his "broken rod" proceeded from the same quarter. Some eastern conqueror has fallen, whose death excites in the Philistines vain hopes of liberation. Now, the death of Tiglath-Pileser III, who annexed Palestine to the Assyrian empire, nearly coincided with that of Ahaz of Judah (727). He was succeeded in turn by Shalmaneser IV and Sargon, by both of whom Philistia was severely scourged. Other interpreters, reading the dates differently, assign the oracle to the end of Shalmaneser's reign (722), or even Sargon's (705). It was the ordinary thing for the death of an Assyrian ruler to be followed by risings in the provinces (see pp. 14, 51, 99). Ewald thought indeed that the "broken rod" of ver. 29 was that of *Judæan* rule, which had become so feeble under Ahaz and is to be replaced for the Philistines by the incomparably harsher domination of Asshur. But ver. 29 assumes that the new tyranny will spring from "the root" of the old, and Judæan ascendency had already for some time been replaced in Philistia by Assyrian when Ahaz died. The year of this king's death was critical for all the nationalities of Palestine.

The warning given to "the messengers" of Philistia is no doubt designed for the benefit of Judæan politicians, who were under severe temptation, through Egyptian intrigues and Philistine example, to join in abortive movements against the Assyrian Government. These seductions Isaiah uniformly opposed. He promises now that while Philistia will be made to "howl" in the coming distress, God's people, notwithstanding their present reduced condition, will remain in safety and Zion will prove an undisturbed "refuge" for her children. This promise was fulfilled through the greater part of Hezekiah's reign, and so long as the Divinely guided policy of Isaiah was followed.

7. *Against Tyre* (or *Zidon?*), chap. 23.—After the oracle against Philistia, not unsuitably, follows "the burden of Tyre." This *massa'* stands last in the series of prophecies forming the Second Book; but it belonged to a comparatively early period. The great encounter between Assyria and Phœnicia, which crippled Tyre's maritime forces, took place in the reign of

Shalmaneser IV (727-722),[1] when Zidon, with the lesser towns of the coast, fell; but Tyre, secure in her island fortress, bore successfully a five years' siege. It was in the course of the same war between Assyria and the western states that Samaria was captured and the kingdom of Northern Israel destroyed (722). Vv. 1-14 are, in fact, a dirge over the fall of *Zidon* (vv. 2. 4), an elegy of high poetic merit, and (with some touches of a later restoring or adapting hand) composed in Isaiah's dialect and manner. It consists of three strophes : 1b-5, 6-9, 10-14. As head of the Phœnician confederacy and mistress of the seas, Tyre was heavily struck in the blow that fell on Zidon ; she was herself at the same time in sore straits, and reports of her approaching fall had gone abroad (vv. 5. 8). "Tarshish" signifies either Tartessus in Spain or the Tyrrhenian (Etruscan) coast of Italy. "The land of Kittim"

[1] So Josephus, *Antiq.*, ix. 14, who quotes here the Greek historian Menander. Some recent Assyriologists, however, assign the fall of Zidon and five years' siege of Tyre to the reign of Sennacherib (701-696), supposing Josephus to have mistaken the one Assyrian king for the other. G. A. Smith prefers this date for the prophecy; Duhm and Marti (*Handkommentar* and *Kurzer Hand-commentar*), amongst the latest commentators, assert that no such complete prostration of the Phœnician power as this poem describes took place until the reign of the Persian king Artaxerxes Ochus in 348 B.C., who burnt Zidon to the ground.

is almost certainly Cyprus, which Sargon a little later claims to have held in tribute. The word "Chaldæans," in ver. 13, is now thought to be a copyist's error for "Canaanites" (Phœnicians).

The Phœnician cities appear to have taken part repeatedly in the western revolts against Assyria, and were punished accordingly. But this calamity is described as falling on Zidon and Tyre at the height of their glory, when the Tyrian empire of the seas was hitherto unbroken. The position of Tyre made her one of the strongest fortresses of antiquity. She defied Nebuchadrezzar for thirteen years (to this famous siege Ezekiel devotes chs. 26–28 of his prophecies, making a reference to its failure in 29 18); though often attacked, she was only captured when Alexander the Great in 332 B.C. threw a mole across the arm of the sea parting island Tyre from the mainland.

The funeral elegy over Zidon terminates with ver. 14, which repeats the opening strain: "Wail, ye ships of Tarshish, for your stronghold is laid waste!" Vv. 15-18 are an addition to the original poem, a postscript written in prose (with the exception of ver. 16), of a different stamp from the foregoing and bearing reference to *Tyre* alone. Interpreters are at variance in their opinion of the date of this paragraph, and its relation to the rest of the chapter. The conjecture of Ewald (followed by Kittel and others), who identifies the "seventy years" of ver. 17 with the period (symbolically) assigned to the Chaldæan ascendency in Jer. 25 11, 12., etc., and Zech. 1 12, and who sees in the last clause of ver. 18 an allusion to the distressing poverty of the Jews on their return from the exile (see Hag. 2 3, Zech. 4 10 8 10-12, Ps. 132 15), supplies the most plausible explanation. Under the Chaldæan empire Phœnician commerce, which had recovered from the disasters of the eighth century, as Ezek. 26–28 shows, again suffered severely, through the desperate and protracted struggle with Nebuchadrezzar and the rivalry of Babylon. It revived once more in the Persian times.

> At that period [the time of the return from Babylon], when the new Jerusalem was very poor and in necessitous circumstances, and the Messianic hopes were nevertheless excited in a high degree, the anticipation and wish expressed in ver. 18 are quite intelligible (Ewald).

We may, therefore, put down this remarkable supplement to some prophetic contemporary of Haggai and Zechariah, who wished well to Tyrian trade and expected that the struggling Judæans and their sanctuary would profit from its revival.

8. *Against Egypt and Ethiopia*, chap. 20.—

Considerably later than the last described falls the second dated prophecy of this book, which is the first of a series directed against Egypt (see chs. 19, 30, 31). "In the year that the Tartan [the Assyrian Commander-in-chief] came unto Ashdod, when Sargon, the king of Asshur, sent him, he fought against Ashdod and took it." Here we find ourselves on chronological *terra firma*. The oracle is singular amongst Isaiah's prophecies, in the fact that he accompanies the inspired word with a symbolic and dramatic act, "walking naked and barefoot, for a sign and a wonder upon Egypt and upon Cush," by way of representing the calamity destined to fall upon these nations at the hands of the Assyrians; for similar actions on the part of prophets, see Jer. 13 1-11 19 1-13, 27, 28, 1 Kings 11 29. 32 22 11. etc. Such violent means Isaiah was compelled to adopt in order to combat the pro-Egyptian movement at Jerusalem, and to prevent his people being enticed into the fatal conspiracy against Assyria once more set on foot.

The Assyrian annals date the siege and capture of Ashdod in the eleventh year of Sargon, 711 B.C. This Philistine city had revolted at the prompting of the Egyptians, who left it in the lurch. It is possible that Egyptian and Ethiopian prisoners were captured at Ashdod;

but there was no invasion of Egypt, nor any extensive captivity from that quarter at this period—not, indeed, until the conquest of Egypt by Esarhaddon forty years later, when the scene here anticipated was realised (see pp. 173-175). For "three years," it is stated, the high-born prophet made his public appearances (probably at intervals) in the shameful guise described. The capture of Ashdod seems to have been the concluding act of this war; the prophecy was therefore first delivered in 714 or 713, at the time when the Egyptian overtures which proved so disastrous to Ashdod and, but for Isaiah, might have been equally fatal to Jerusalem, were first made.

It is to be observed that ch. 20, like chs. 36-39 (but unlike the dated ch. 6), is an historical piece, and refers to Isaiah in the *third* person. It has the appearance of being extracted from some biographical source.

9. *Against Moab.* — Next in order comes a group of three oracles, probably synchronous, bearing on *Moab*, *Edom*, and *Dedan* (*Arabia*). Isaiah's "burden of Moab" (chs. 15, 16) we discussed in Vol. I, Ch. VI, regarding it as the legacy of a previous age which this prophet has adopted and applied to contemporary Moab in the concluding sentences of ch. 16 13. 14: "This is the

word that Jehovah spake concerning Moab in time past. But now Jehovah hath spoken, saying, Within three years, as the years of an hireling " (who makes his day's work as short as he may; comp. 21 16), "and the glory of Moab will be brought into contempt with all his great multitude, and the remnant will be very small and of no account." The prophet's threatening is closely similar to that used against "Ephraim" in ch. 17 4-6 (see pp. 61–62 above). To which Assyrian invasion of Isaiah's time the words refer, it is impossible to say. The advice addressed to Moab in ch. 16 1 seems to point to Hezekiah's reign, when the Judæan Government was in such power that it might, conceivably, have looked for tribute to the Trans-Jordanic clans, which in earlier times had been tributary to the king of Northern Israel (see Vol. I, p. 118). Assyrian inscriptions refer to Moabite submission under Tiglath-Pileser in 734, and under Sennacherib in 701. The first of these dates is too early, the second too late, to suit the condition just specified. But Moab may very well have been overrun by the Assyrians, though the fact is unnoticed in the extant Annals, during the Shalmaneser-Sargon campaigns of 724–720 in Palestine, or the later Sargon campaign of 711. The analogous expression which occurs in the dated prophecy of ch. 20 (ver. 3: "three years") suggests the last of the above-mentioned occasions; and we assign, conjecturally, Isaiah's republication of the ancient "burden of Moab" to the period antecedent to the year 711, when an Egyptian and Philistine conspiracy against the Assyrian suzerain was hatched, which Sargon was preparing to crush by an invasion of Palestine. Into this alliance, it seems likely, Moab was being drawn, against the warning of Judah (see, on this crisis, pp. 13-14, 76-77). A detachment from Sargon's army, sent against Philistia and Egypt (20 1), would suffice to quell the Moabite rising.

10. *Against Edom (Dumah)*, chap. 21 11. 12.— The Aramaisms of the "Dumah" burden (a feature common to it with chs. 15, 16), together with its pregnant and enigmatic form, indicate an antique and pre-Isaianic origin; as Ewald observed—followed by Dillmann, König, and others—this utterance, in vv. 11b. 12a, resembles nothing so much as an old pithy response to Edom, which is repeated for the occasion. Many interpreters connect this oracle with the foregoing (vv. 1-11, *Against Babylon*) because of their juxtaposition, and because in both the prophet figures as a "watchman" (see vv. 6. 8); but the Hebrew word rendered *watchman* differs in these passages,

and the sentence upon Edom is still more akin to that upon *Dedan* (vv. 13 ff.), which is unmistakably linked to the oracle against *Moab* (chs. 15, 16). The resemblance of vv. 11. 12 to vv. 6 and 8 may have determined the order adopted by the compiler. The question, "Watchman, what time of night?" (literally, "how much of the night?") is imagined as coming from a sleeper indoors, who is roused by the cry of the watchman pacing the street. The answer is so vague as to be almost mocking—"Morning cometh, and also night"; the consulter of the prophet is told in the last clause of ver. 12, that he may get better instruction if he inquires again later. "Night" is commonly taken to symbolize calamity for the Edomites; but it may be doubted whether the question means more than our colloquialism, "what time of day?" ("how are things going?") The *Dumah* of the title may be a copyist's error for *Edom* (so in the Septuagint); or else it is a play upon the word *Edom* (turning this into *Silence*), which indicates humorously the uninforming gist of the response.

11. *Against the Dedanites*, ch. 21 13-17.—In "the burden upon Arabia" we have a terse and vivid oracle for the caravans of the *Dedanim*, an Arabian tribe in whose hands lay the traffic which passed eastwards and southwards from

Phœnicia across the Syrian desert. "Kedar" (16. 17) is a wider name for the North Arabian peoples, who are warned at large, in terms resembling those addressed to Damascus and Ephraim in ch. 17 and to Moab in ch. 16 13. 14, of their impending desolation. Such calamity, in Isaiah's time, could only proceed from Assyrian invaders. The prediction of ver. 16, "Within a year, according to the years of an hireling (see p. 78), and all the glory of Kedar shall fail," is so nearly identical with the warning of Moab in 16 14 that the two can hardly have been remote in time. When the prophet now says "within *a year*," instead of "three years" as in 16 14, one must either suppose that this forecast was later than the other, or else (with Duhm) that the numeral *three* has accidentally dropped out of this text. It is conjectured, for reasons similar to those given in the former instance, that ver. 14 quotes an old saying about the hospitality of Teyma'—a famous Arabian town (referred to in Job 6 19) lying far southeast in the desert—to which the prophet gives his own sad application in ver. 15. The word "Arabia" in ver. 13, suggesting the title,[1] is

---

[1] This title is wanting in the Septuagint text of ver. 13; the Greeks appear to have read vv. 11-17 as one continuous prophecy.

doubtful in point of text; the Greek translators, vocalising the Hebrew letters differently, rendered them "(thou shalt lodge) *in the evening*"; "in the steppe" is probably the correct rendering: the merchants with their train of camels must avoid the usual halting-places, where the enemy will be in ambush awaiting them, and encamp in the desert thickets. The geographical term *Arabia* was, most likely, of a later origin.

The Assyrian expedition against Moab, which Isaiah appears to foresee in ch. 16, would inevitably threaten the trade-routes of the Dedanite merchants. Doubtless the Edomites, with their port of Elath at the head of the Red Sea, were endangered in the projected Assyrian campaign. If so, chs. 15-16, 21 11. 12 and 21 13-17 relate to the same crisis. The three oracles may have been addressed in turn to representatives of these neighbouring peoples at Hezekiah's court (comp. 18 2), who had come for consultation with a view to concerted action against the Assyrian overlord, at a time when rebellion was simmering throughout Syria and Palestine (see p. 79).

12. *Concerning Cush*, chap. 18.—This most interesting prophecy belongs to a quite definite situation. It is addressed to the "ambassadors" (comp. 14 32 21 11 30 4; and see pp. 12-13) of

Ethiopia (Hebrew *Cush*), the region of the Upper Nile where the great stream parts into "rivers" (vv. 1. 2), now peopled by the Nubians and Soudanese. Isaiah well describes them as "a people tall and smooth" (or "shining"), "and terrible [in war] from their beginning"; their appearance must have made a sensation in Jerusalem. The Ethiopians were politically masters of Egypt through great part of the eighth century; after an interval of dispossession, they appear to have reconquered the country during the troubles which ensued on the defeat of the Egyptians by Sargon in the year 720 (see Vol. I, pp. 239–240). Their ambassadors had arrived at Jerusalem, presumably to concert measures against the Assyrians; and the prophet, addressing them in a friendly tone, gives them a message which, sent to so distant and wide-ruling a people, seemed to be designed for "all the inhabitants of the world" (3). These imposing strangers, representing an imperial Government, are told that Jehovah will Himself "cut off the shoots" of the invader's power "before the harvest" and "cut down his spreading branches" (ver. 5; comp. 10 33. 34), leaving the enemy's hosts to be a prey to "ravenous birds" (6). This victory gained by Jehovah of hosts, unaided, over the common foe is to be honoured by "a present brought unto" Him at Mount Zion. The passage ends, in ver. 7, with the same graphic description of the Ethiopians and their country with which it began—a delineation that bespeaks Isaiah's wide knowledge of foreign peoples and lands.[1]

The *rapprochement* between the Ethiopian dynasty of Egypt and Judæa may have taken place antecedently to the war either of 711 or 701. Most probably it was connected with the latter; it was at this epoch that Isaiah entertained the clear and confident expectation of the overthrow of the Assyrians in conflict with Israel that is here expressed. In the crisis of 711 Isaiah predicted the victory of Assyria (ch. 20; see p. 76 above). This oracle was therefore somewhat earlier than those of chs. 30–37.

13. *Concerning Egypt*, chap. 19.—"The burden of Egypt" is perhaps the most extraordinary—

[1] Cush is called, in ver. 1, "the land of the whirring [*or* rustling, *or* clanging] of wings." The Hebrew *tsiltsal* is obscure. Delitzsch and Kittel think it refers to the tsetse-fly of Central Africa, of whose dreaded power Isaiah may have heard. Others take it to be a general expression for the buzz of winged insect-life that fills the Nile valley. A tempting explanation is that of Knobel, favoured by Dillmann,—*land of the double shadow* or *shadow on both sides* (*tsel* is Hebrew for *shadow*), describing the fact that in the tropics the sun casts its shadow now north and now south. The report of this would cause extreme wonder in men of northern latitudes.

it is certainly the most catholic and far-sighted of Isaiah's prophecies. It predicts the subjection of the land of Egypt to "a cruel lord and a fierce king" (ver. 4), due to cowardice and internal strife (1.2) and to the folly and ill-counsel resulting from idolatry (vv. 3. 11-15), a calamity aggravated by failure of the Nile-flood and the suspension of industry (vv. 5-8). The *Assyrians* are not mentioned in this picture of disaster; but the reference in vv. 23-25 (assuming the unity of the chapter) implies that they are the oppressors foreseen in ver. 4; otherwise, an Ethiopian conqueror might have been supposed to be intended by the "fierce king" of that passage.

In Egypt's humiliation, she is to turn to Jehovah of hosts. His worship will be established in five of her cities, and "a pillar" (obelisk) set up to Him "at her border" (vv. 18. 19). Vv. 20-22 (comp. Obad. 21, Hos. 6 1-3) describe the repentance and salvation of Egypt in language such as might have been applied to Israel herself Finally Israel appears, in vv. 23. 24, as allied in peaceful confederation with Egypt and Assyria, supplying a bond of union and a religious centre for the two imperial powers; and the prophecy closes with the benediction, "Blessed be Egypt My people, and Assyria the work of My hands, and Israel My inheritance."

It is difficult to understand a picture like this as drawn in Isaiah's time; it is still more difficult to account for it as originating in any later age of Judaism before the Christian era. Vv. 16-25 are written in a more prosaic style than the foregoing, and vv. 18-25 breathe a goodwill toward Egypt, and finally toward Assyria, hitherto unexampled in Isaiah; but the prophecy taken as a whole, with the qualification made below, is continuous and logically connected, while vv. 1-15 are decidedly Isaianic in linguistic and stylistic character, as well as in the political situation they presuppose. The five supplementary paragraphs beginning with the phrase "in that day," remind us of vv. 10 and 11-16 of ch. 11 (see p. 54); and the same judgement must be passed on these sections as on those. The interpreters who insist on the post-Isaianic authorship of these clauses, see in "Asshur" (vv. 23-25) an archaic expression for Persia, or for the Græco-Syrian kingdom of the third century B.C. Ver. 18 is under strong suspicion of being an exilic interpolation due to the settlement of Jews in Egypt; but the number "five" probably signifies "a few" (as in 17 6 30 17, etc.), and it was quite natural, according to ancient ideas—the suzerainty of Jehovah in Egypt being once acknowledged—to suppose that "cities" would be assigned to Him in the subject territory. The last clause of this verse, which gives (with various readings) a definite *city-name* in this connexion, may very well be a gloss upon the Hebrew text, added in the time of Jewish settlement by way of confirming the prediction.

Egypt was at last invaded and completely conquered by Esarhaddon and Asshurbanipal in the years 670-664 (see pp. 173-175): to such conquest the prophet looks forward in vv. 1-4; the distracted condition of the country and the ineptitude of its policy made the event inevitable; Isaiah evidently counted upon it sooner than it actually happened. For some twenty years Egypt remained crushed beneath the heel of the "cruel lord" of Nineveh. But for thirty years before this, in the interval between Sennacherib's overthrow and his son's invasion of Egypt, there was a lull in the chronic struggle; the little kingdom of Judah was left untroubled, and the highway from Egypt to Assyria, skirting its borders, was trodden only by peaceful traffickers. In the early years of that interval Isaiah's life-work, commenced in 740 (see 6 1) two generations earlier, came to its close, and vv. 23-25 are probably his last extant utterance.

"We can hardly imagine," said Dr Cheyne in his Commentary, "a more swan-like end for a dying prophet." His mind returns to the grand conception of his people's missionary calling with which it first set out. In his youth, Isaiah sang of "the mountain of Jehovah's house exalted above the hills" and "all nations flowing unto it"; of the peoples "beating their swords into ploughshares, their spears into pruninghooks," and "learning war no more" (2 2-4). After so many wars, so many thunderings of judgement and bursts of anger and scorn against both Egypt and Assyria for their wrongs done to Israel, his last words breathe reconciliation; his eyes close upon the vision of "Israel the third with Egypt and Assyria, a blessing in the midst of the earth." Isaiah proves himself to the end at once the most spiritual, and the most political and practical of Israel's teachers. His dying prophecy, which still remains to be fulfilled, is that of a universal peace amongst the great powers of the world, established by the rule of Jehovah and secured by a common and hearty allegiance to the Holy One of Israel.

C.—Post-Isaianic Oracles

There remain, out of the fifteen pieces contained in Book II of Isaiah, only the first and the tenth, chs. 13 2-14 23 and 21 1-10, both relating to Babylon, which bear unmistakable signs of a non-Isaianic situation and handiwork.

14. *On the Fall of Babylon*, chap. 21 1-10.—The earlier of the two oracles against Babylon bears the obscure title, "the burden of the wilderness of the sea," where "the wilderness" is suggested by ver. 1; and "of the sea" (a qualification wanting in the Greek Version) is probably intended to define the desert over which the storm sweeps down upon Babylon as that lying at the head of the Persian Gulf and separating Chaldæa from "Elam" eastwards. This geographical outlook, if correctly determined, suggests at the outset a Chaldæan habitat for the writer.

Thrice at least in Isaiah's time, according to the cuneiform inscriptions, was Babylon taken and sacked by the Assyrians, after unsuccessful revolt—in the years 710, 703, and 696; it was natural to think that one or other of these calamities gave occasion to the elegy. So, amongst other historical critics, Drs Driver (in *Life and Times of Isaiah* ed. 1), Cheyne (*The Prophecies of Isaiah* ed. 3), and G. A. Smith (*Expositor's Bible*) had supposed, understanding Isaiah to be actuated by sympathy for fallen Babylon (comp. 39 1.2) on account of the common hatred toward Assyria. But each of these scholars has reverted to the older critical view established by Ewald, that ch. 21, like chs. 13 and 14, can only refer to the conquest of Babylon by Cyrus. No Babylonian catastrophe happening in the age of Hezekiah could have been watched with the strained and passionate expectation here implied.

> It is incredible that Isaiah should have taken such interest in the subjugation of Babylon by Sargon, and received the news of this with anguish and dismay (3. 4); the tireless opponent of all foreign alliances, he cannot have regarded this catastrophe as the overthrow of an ally (see ch. 39), and vv. 8 and 9 exhibit the seer as long expecting the event, and rejoicing in the downfall it brings for the Babylonian gods (Kittel).

The assailants summoned are "Elam" and "Media" (2)—as much as to say, "the Persians and Medes"; for it is now certain that Cyrus, though Persian in origin, commenced his career as king of *Elam*;[1] he annexed Media and then assailed Babylon in this character. Elamites were found, indeed, amongst the Assyrian troops of the eighth century (22 6); but it is not likely that Medes served in this way, whereas the terms of ver. 2 precisely describe the forces of Cyrus.

This prophecy we must therefore associate with chs. 13, 14, and 40 ff., as belonging to the time of the Exile and of the rise of Cyrus; and

---

[1] See Hastings' *Dict. of Bible* on "Elam."

we shall have occasion to notice it again in that connexion (Vol. IV). The author views the ruin of Babylon from a standpoint of his own—neither with the fierce exultation which animates chs. 13, 14, nor with the rapturous hope for restored Israel that inspired the writer of chs. 40–52. He looks on the scene with the eyes of the poet and the student of history, rather than of the Judæan patriot; he is awestruck by the sudden and tragic doom overtaking the great world-city, and by the convulsion in human affairs he is witnessing; he hangs pondering and in suspense over the issue of this tremendous downfall. He writes, presumably, at an earlier date than his fellow-prophets of the same era, and when Cyrus was first threatening Babylon, as he did eleven years before its final occupation in 538. The vision is prophetical, and not composed *post eventum*. The doom pronounced is certain, being fixed in the counsels of God and approaching in the swift current of events. It was a mistake to ascribe to the writer, on the strength of vv. 3 and 4, a compassion for Babylon, which the last clause of ver. 10 quite excludes. The oracle is highly imaginative, and dramatic in conception and form. Its style approaches Isaiah's sufficiently to account for the identification; but is more abrupt and laconic, and exhibits several expressions of a later stamp. In vv. 1 and 3 the poet reminds us of Nahum; in vv. 6-10 he resembles Habakkuk.

15. *Against Babylon*, ch. 13 2-14 23.—The title, "the burden of Babylon," carries the addition— taken over, probably, from the First Book (1 1) as appropriate by way of heading to the Second Book of this prophet—" which Isaiah, the son of Amoz, did see." Such a designation can hardly have been given to the *massa'* on its own account simply, nor until the tradition of its origin was lost (comp. pp. 12, 95-96, 124-126). Contents, language, allusions, the standpoint of the writer, the tone and spirit of the composition— all essential considerations go to claim for the brilliant author (or authors) of this pæan a place in the circle of the unknown prophets who hailed from Babylon the advent of Cyrus, who were the forerunners of the return from the Exile and the morning stars of Israel's new day of spiritual glory. Franz Delitzsch, in the last (fourth) edition of his great Commentary, surrendered, as in the case of chs. 40-66, the traditional view of the authorship, frankly accepting the exilic date.[1]

---

[1] Dr C. von Orelli, whose excellent Commentary has been translated into English, is almost the only scholar of note who still asserts the full Isaianic authorship of this "burden."

The situation presupposed is not that of Isaiah's day. The Jews are not warned, as Isaiah might have warned them (39 6), against the folly of concluding an alliance with Babylon, or reminded of the disastrous consequences which such an alliance might entail ; nor are they threatened, as Jeremiah might have threatened them, with impending exile : they are represented as *in exile*, and as about to be delivered from it (14 1. 2). It was the office of the prophet of Israel to address himself to the needs of his own age, to announce to his contemporaries the judgements and consolations which arose out of the circumstances of their own time, to interpret for them their own history. To base a promise upon a condition of things *not yet existent*, and without any point of contact with the circumstances or situation of those to whom it is addressed, would be alien to the genius of prophecy. Upon grounds of analogy, the prophecy of 13 2–14 23 can only be attributed to an author living towards the close of the Exile and holding out to his contemporaries the prospect of release from Babylon, as Isaiah held out to his contemporaries the prospect of deliverance from Assyria.[1]

At most it might be feasible, as Dr. H. Strack attempts,[2] to vindicate for Isaiah ch. 13 2-13, verses of a general tenor,—supposed to be an isolated fragment of the old prophet, which a successor

[1] S. R. Driver, *Introduction to the Literature of the Old Testament*, p. 201.
[2] In his concise and judicious *Einleitung an das A.T.*, p. 82.

in the Exile has worked up into a new oracle suited to encourage the Israel of his day. This explanation would indeed save the historicity of the title; but it robs Isaiah of everything distinctive in the prophecy; at the same time, there are decided objections to claiming for him the opening paragraphs in question. Reading "the burden of Babylon" in the sense we have maintained, we hold it over for examination at a later stage of this work, along with ch. 21 1-10 (see the last section).

APPENDIX

CHS. 24–27 are of a character sensibly different from those which precede and those which follow them. They form a continuous prophetic poem, which looks beyond the historical conditions of the Israelite kingdoms and the national struggle, to anticipate a final "day of Jehovah" affecting the destiny of "all peoples." This is the beginning, in fact, of a new style of prophecy which terminates in the Apocalypse of St John, and which had a rich development in Jewish literature in the period between 200 B.C. and 100 A.D. This Apocalypse supplies a summary conclusion to the Oracles of Isaiah (and others) against the Foreign Nations, being a prophecy of *world-judgement*, in which all the nations together will participate; so much is intimated by the opening sentence of ch. 24: "Behold, Jehovah doth empty out *the earth*, and maketh it bare" (comp. vv. 3-6, 13-15). The Third Book of Isaiah, chs. 28–33, is similarly rounded off by the addition of chs. 34, 35 (see p. 124); and ch. 12 we judged to be a post-Isaianic conclusion, of a slighter nature, appended to Book I (see p. 54).

In sublimity and force of conception these four chapters are worthy of the greatest of the prophets; but they have no real point of contact with Isaiah's times: ch. 27 13 presumes the national exile as already matter of history; the one definite reference made to the enemies of Israel, viz. to *Moab* in 25 10. 11, is opposite in tone to the oracle of chs. 15, 16. While Isaianic phrases and figures meet us frequently in this poem (see 24 13. 19 25 2. 7 26 20 27 2 ff. 9. 10. 13), it betrays the influence of later writers also—Nahum, Jeremiah, Ezekiel, Haggai, and the author of Ps. 118—along with Joel, Amos, and Hosea. The author's style and method are not those of Isaiah. He is a lyrical poet and visionary, not a preacher and orator; he ranks with the Psalmists as much as with the Prophets. His representations are abstract and idealistic, not to say grandiose—vague in drawing, and with the colours dashed broadly on the canvas; we miss the clear outline, the delicate characterization and firm grasp of the concrete, that distinguish Isaiah's work alike in description of the present and prediction of the future. The doctrine of the Resurrection unfolded in chs. 25 7. 8 and 26 19 belongs to a later, perhaps a much later stage of Old Testament revelation; it goes far beyond that of Hos. 13 14 (see Vol. I, p.182). The whole composition breathes another atmosphere and belongs to another world than that of the seventh century.

The vagueness of the writing, and the absence in it of historical allusion, make its date uncertain; some critics refer it to the sixth or beginning of the fifth century (to exilic or early post-exilic times: so Ewald, Riehm, Delitzsch, Dillmann, Kittel); others to the fourth century and the convulsions attending the reign of Artaxerxes Ochus and the rise of the Greek dominion (so Smend, Stade, Marti); while Duhm and Cheyne bring it down as late as the second century B.C. and the epoch of John Hyrcanus! In any case, the prophecy witnesses to a period of Israel's life and thought long subsequent to that which we are now reviewing; we shall find a place in our last Volume for its consideration.

CHAPTER XVI

THE LATER PROPHECIES OF ISAIAH:
CHAPTERS XXVIII–XXXIII

The Third Book of Isaiah—The Nucleus in chs. 29-31—Isaiah's Policy in the War with Sennacherib—The Lesson of Ephraim's Ruin — Situation of Samaria—The Northern and Southern Capitals—The "Covenant with Death"—Necromancy—Proverbial Strain in Isaiah—"Woe to Ariel"—Blindness to the National Crisis—Secret Treaty with Egypt—Hollowness of Egyptian Promises—Isaiah bidden to *write*—Impeachment of Judæan Government — Israel's coming Glory — The Assyrian's coming Doom—Zion's True Protector—Another Picture of the Messianic Times—Rebuke of the Women of Jerusalem—A Glance into the Future—Jerusalem's Redemption through Suffering—"Zion a Quiet Habitation"—Authorship of ch. 33—Origin of chs. 34, 35—Outlook of ch. 34—The Historical Appendix (chs. 36-39).

REACHING chap. 28, we find ourselves again within the horizon of the eighth century and catch the unmistakable notes of Isaiah's voice. The six chapters here beginning form a compact whole; they consist of six discourses, bearing the marks of oral delivery, which are distinguished by the chapter-divisions, except that vv. 1-8 of ch. 32 belong to 31. The five principal orations—excluding 32 9-20 (the connexion of which is doubtful)—begin each of them with the cry, "Woe to —— !" (comp. the great philippic of 5 8-25 10 1-4; see pp. 36–37), indicating a unity of structure in the series of addresses which corresponds to its singleness of aim. The scope of this Third Book of Isaiah is well defined by Dillmann:

> A circle of Discourses, in which the wonderful plan of God in His dealings with Zion is unfolded, in opposition to the false schemes of the political leaders at Jerusalem.

Chap. 28, which originated much earlier, is introductory to the main subject; and ch. 33 is supplementary. This last speech betrays the hand of some scholar of Isaiah (see pp. 123–124 below), who may have finished off and published the entire Book (28-33) for the edification of the rescued Jerusalem. At a later epoch chs. 34 and 35 were appended to this collection (comp. p. 94 ff. above), possibly not until the time when the three Books of Isaiah (1-11, 13-23, 28-33) were combined in the single volume (1-39) inscribed with his name, to which thereafter the great supplement of chs. 40–66 was attached.

Chaps. 29–31 form therefore the kernel of this Book. They bear on the situation caused by the rupture with Assyria and the abortive alliance of the Judæans with Egypt, which took place in the opening years of Sennacherib's reign, 705–701 B.C. Apart from some half-dozen clauses in which glosses or editorial touches are detected by the critics, these chapters reproduce in a pure and well-preserved form Isaiah's speeches made during Hezekiah's rebellion against the Assyrians. Combining with chs. 29–33 ch. 22—"The Oracle of the Valley of Vision," and the Denunciation of Shebna (see pp. 63–67)—which belongs to an early stage in the same war, and the story of the siege of Jerusalem as given in the historical conclusion to "Isaiah" (chs. 36, 37), we have before us a full view of this critical epoch. At this point Isaiah's ministry of forty years culminated; the spirit of prophecy in him maintained a victorious conflict on the one hand with the popular infidelity represented by the Egyptian party at Hezekiah's court (see pp. 12–13, 76), and on the other hand with the overwhelming and haughty heathen empire of Assyria. Deserted by Egypt and brought to penitent shame by their desperate condition, Hezekiah and Jerusalem found salvation in the sole might of Jehovah's wonder-working arm. Jehovah's people were thus taught the most signal lesson inculcated upon them since the Exodus and the victories of David (see Pss. 46 and 48, for the *moral* of the occasion).

Isaiah's policy and attitude during the war with Sennacherib were the same that he assumed thirty years before in his dealings with Ahaz. Now, as then, he denounces all dependence upon heathen powers. He declares that through the invaders Jehovah means to punish His disloyal people, but will in the last extremity defend His city, and will save Zion when she has been cleansed through judgement. The affronted majesty of "the Holy One of Israel," and the inviolability of Zion—these were the key-notes of Isaiah's ministry first and last. In 734 the Assyrians were Judah's foreign allies, whose help Ahaz sought against his neighbours; in 704 they are the oppressors and "treacherous dealers" whose lordship, endured for a generation, Judah attempts to throw off, with the vainly expected help of Egypt. Formerly king Ahaz, the apostate son of David, bore the brunt of condemnation, since he was personally responsible for calling in the help of Assyria: it is noticeable that Hezekiah is not mentioned in these chapters, unless it be in the promise of 33 17; we are led to suppose that the criminal policy proceeded from "the princes," the "men of scorn" ruling in Jerusalem (28 14 30 1-5)—with perhaps the foreigner Shebna, so bitterly denounced in 22 15ff., for a leading spirit amongst them—and that the king, whom Isaiah spares, was overborne by his nobility; in ch. 39, however, Hezekiah is himself censured. On the godless politicians, with their shallow worldly wisdom and their recourse to necromancy and magic arts, Isaiah pours the vials of Jehovah's wrath. The rescuer invited by Ahaz in 734 had interposed, only too effectually—Jehovah fetched him from the ends of the earth, but his help meant Israel's subjugation and despoliation; the ally now invoked will prove nothing but "a shame and a reproach" (30 5). By way of contrast to Ahaz, Isaiah had delineated the ideal Son of David whom God will one day enthrone in Zion (9 6.7); here the Messiah-king is not forgotten (see 32 1 33 17), but it is the vision of a regenerated people and a peaceful, thriving land on which the prophet's gaze is fixed—a condition of things the opposite to that which now prevails (29 22-24 30 19-26 32 1-8. 16-19 33 5. 6. 17-24). These idealistic traits of description many critics credit, in whole or part, to a later hand. Let us review the several prophecies that make up this third and last Book of the original Isaiah:—

1. *The ruin of Ephraim and its lesson for Zion*, chap. 28.—Vv. 1-6 carry us back to a time antedating the fall of Samaria, to the early years of Isaiah's preaching; this oracle is contemporary with 9 8-21 in the First Book, and with 17 1-11 in the Second (see pp. 36, 61-63). It is complete in itself, and counts amongst the finest passages of Isaiah's oratory. The prophecy concludes with a promise for *Judah*, which we can only refer to the epoch of religious reformation at the outset of Hezekiah's reign (see pp. 20-22), that "the Lord of hosts will be for a crown of glory and for a diadem of beauty unto the residue of His people, and for a spirit of judgement" to their rulers, "and for strength" to their warriors (vv. 5. 6). For a moment this had seemed possible to Isaiah in the immediate future, despite the stern commission he was at first charged with (6 9-13). But the happy vision is recalled by the prophet only that he may express, in language of extreme disgust (vv. 7. 8), his disenchantment: "But these also [*the residue* above referred to] reel through wine, and stagger through strong drink. . . . All tables are full of filthy vomit";

comp. 5 11 ff. 22 ff., Amos 6 3-6, Hosea 7 5, for similar traits.

"The crown of pride" worn by "the drunkards of Ephraim," "the fading flower of his splendid array, which is on the head of the fat valley," is a figure depicting the city of *Samaria* as she stood in her glory—on a rounded hill of great natural strength, commanding a rich dale spread out in corn- and vine-lands, down which it looked westwards to the plain of Sharon and the sea, its summit girt with turreted walls and surmounted by palaces and temples, while orchards and gardens covered the lower slopes. In the distance Samaria shone like a coronal of flowers upon some fair head—a garland wreathing, alas, *a drunkard's brow*! The head that wears it will sink under the coming storm; the gay flowers shall be trampled in the mire (2-4). This prophecy of evil belongs to the time before the siege of Samaria by Shalmaneser, and after the accession of Hezekiah—*circa* 725 B.C. (see Vol. I, p. 122, and pp. 10–11 above).

The connexion between vv. 1 6 and 7-22 lies in the thought that the punishment which has *now*—at the date of ver. 7—actually fallen on Samaria, will be extended to *Jerusalem*, since they are alike in guilt; south will suffer with north under the Assyrian scourge. The same moral was drawn by Micah of Moresheth from the overthrow of Samaria (Mic. 1; see Vol. I, pp. 254-256). Isaiah's warning is met with derision by "the men of scorn, who rule this people which is in Jerusalem" (ver. 14) : vv. 9. 10 contain their reply to the prophet,—who treats them, forsooth, like babes, dealing out his stale moralities "line upon line, precept upon precept, here a little and there a little," till they are sick and tired! And vv. 11-13 are his retort upon the scorners, intimating that Jehovah will enforce these despised lessons, the ABC of national duty which the Judæan statesmen have still to learn, by other and stern masters, *in the Assyrian tongue*!

The "covenant with death" and "compact with Sheol" on which the ruling party build, is obscure in its nature; its object is plain, viz. to ward off the Assyrian peril, the "flooding scourge" of vv. 15. 18 (comp. ver. 17, and 8 7, 8, 10 26), against which the men in power at Jerusalem vainly imagine they have ensured the state—in all probability, by means of a secret alliance with *Egypt*.[1] This interpretation brings ch. 28 into connexion with 29-31, which deal explicitly with the Egyptian entanglement. To

---

[1] As to the nature of this compact, see note [1] on p. 38 above.

associate vv. 7-22 with the latest occasion for such alliance (705-1) is to put a space of twenty years between this utterance and that of vv. 1-6; some interval the "But" of ver. 7, with its note of disappointment, evidently implies. Perhaps a middle date is most suitable; in 711[1] the fall of Samaria would be freshly remembered, and chs. 19 1-15, and 20, show that Isaiah at this time was using strong deterrents against confederacy with Egypt. "Lies" were "the refuge" and "falsehood" the "hiding-place" of the friends of Egypt (15), since they were negotiating with the southern power while keeping up a show of loyalty to the Assyrian suzerain. The view of ver. 15 advanced by Duhm and Kittel is, however, plausible; they read the "covenant with *death*" and "agreement with *Sheol*" more literally, as describing necromantic practices, *dealings with the dead*, such as the prophet denounced in the time of Ahaz (8 19). In any case, the latter clauses of vv. 15 and 18 oblige us to look for some crisis when Assyrian invasion seemed imminent, which was the case at each of the three periods in Hezekiah's reign that we have noted.

The apologue of vv. 23-29 shows Isaiah's versa-

[1] For the activity of Egypt, and the temptation of Judah, at this epoch, see pp. 72, 77

tility and accomplishment of style. It is written in the Gnomic or Proverbial strain, characterizing the Chokmah (Wisdom) literature, of ancient use amongst Semitic peoples. The grounds on which certain critics contest its Isaianic authorship are inadequate; ch. 5 1. 2 shows a similar vein in our prophet. The moral of this parable of God's husbandry is not quite obvious. Ver. 26 and ver. 29 appear, in fact, to draw *two* different lessons from the opening and closing acts in the farmer's operations : (*a*) he *ploughs* just so long as need be and *sows* each kind of crop in the plot most suitable, showing herein a wisdom taught him by God, a knowledge of time and situation and material (vv. 23-26) which the would-be-wise statesmen of Judah might well imitate; and (*b*) when the time of *threshing* comes, each sort of grain—harder or softer, coarser or finer—is dealt with by its appropriate instrument, under God's own wonderful direction, who deals in like fashion with men and nations in His manifold discipline, that is always adapted in its method and duration to its specific end (vv. 27-29). Ver. 28 throws a ray of hope upon the dark future hitherto described—" he will not *ever* be threshing it!"

2. *The redemption, through chastisement, of Jerusalem*, ch. 29.—The " Woe " uttered in ch. 29

upon "Ariel,[1] the city where David encamped," is brought within a short distance of the anticipated siege by the words of ver. 1, "Add year to year, let the feasts come round." This may not mean, as many suppose, that definitely within the *next* year Jehovah will "straiten Ariel" (2), but rather (so Duhm and Kittel) that for a year or two more the sacred cycle may run on undisturbed. The turn of expression points to the Harvest Feast (of Tabernacles) at the close of the Jewish year as the occasion of this speech. The siege is portrayed in vv. 3. 4; then vv. 5-8 describe the sudden repulse of the besiegers and the dispersal of "the multitude of all the nations that war against Mount Zion." *Ariel* proves an altar-hearth, for which not Israel but her godless foes will supply the sacrificial victim. Jerusalem's distress, and their triumph, prove alike as a passing dream (7. 8). Thus Isaiah strikes the cheering note prevailing through the Sennacherib crisis (but see pp. 63-64), which was faintly sounded in chap. 28. Vv. 1-8 may be referred without hesitation, and by probable consequence the rest of this chapter, to the year

[1] *Ari-el* (or *-al*) probably denotes *hearth-of-God*, or *altar-hearth*, the hearth on which a great sacrifice will be consumed by fire. Dr Cheyne's suggestion, that the word is a play upon *Uriel*, a supposed synonym for *Urusalem*, the archaic name of Jerusalem, finds favour with scholars.

703 or 702, when events were ripening for Sennacherib's assault upon Jerusalem.

As yet danger seems far off. At the autumn feast the people hear Isaiah's message with astonishment (ver. 9), even as the rulers had received like warnings at an earlier time with contempt (28 9. 14): they are "blind" to their situation; Jehovah has "poured on" them "a spirit of deep sleep" (9. 10); "the vision" is like "a sealed book," which the learned put from them because it is sealed, and the unlearned because they cannot read (11. 12). The hypocrisy of the popular worship (vv. 13. 14; comp. 1 10-17), the crooked policy of the statesmen and their insolent disregard of Jehovah (14-16; comp. 28 14-19), have made this "marvellous work" of judgement necessary and inevitable.[1] Soon there will be a turning upside down of the existing state (17, repeated in 32 15), when the people at present so deaf and blind will "understand" (18); and while the "meek" and "poor" are gladdened with salvation (19), the fierce invaders from without and the "scorners" and false accusers within Israel will alike be brought low (20. 21). Shame and dread toward man will be replaced

[1] The "Woe" of ver. 15 is an echo of that in ver. 1, and does not introduce a new discourse. There is a close and obvious connexion between vv. 14 and 15.

by a holy fear toward Jehovah and a sure understanding of His ways (22-24). The 29th chapter is continuous, and entirely relevant to the national crisis. Only in one or two unimportant phrases need interpolation be suspected. The speech exhibits that blending of threatening and promise —the prospect of heavy chastisement issuing in the signal deliverance of Jerusalem, associated with the hope of moral and material redemption resulting therefrom—which formed the staple of Isaiah's teaching in this last period of his prophetic work.

3. *Denunciation of the treaty with Egypt*, ch. 30.—The third discourse of this Book brings us to the heart of the national crisis. The deep-laid plot of the Judæan Government, which it would fain "hide from Jehovah," this "work" which they "have wrought in a dark place" saying, "who seeth us?" (29 15. 16), has come to light. The secret negotiations between Hezekiah's ministers and the court of Pharaoh are completed, and an embassy bearing princely gifts is now on its way across the desert to Zoan (Tanis) and Hanes (Heracleopolis), at that time the capital cities of Lower Egypt (vv. 4-6).[1] "The

[1] The title at the head of ver. 6, "The oracle of the beasts of the South country" (*i.e.* the *Negeb*, the half-desert region in the south of Judæa bordering upon the Sinaitic peninsula),

land of trouble and anguish" through which the ambassadors are travelling, images the fate of their enterprise. For this confederacy, now openly contracted in defiance of the Assyrian over-lord, has been made without consulting Jehovah—nay, in contempt of His declared will (vv. 1. 2); "therefore shall the strength of Pharaoh be your shame, and the trust in the shadow of Egypt your confusion" (3).

With keen political insight Isaiah stigmatizes the Egyptian state in the enigmatic words of ver. 7: "Yea, as for the Egyptians, their help is mere breath and emptiness! therefore I designate their land *Rachab the sluggard*!" "Rachab," i.e. *impetuous violence*, is taken to be the name of a mythical sea-monster in Semitic antiquity, and the word had become a symbolic epithet of Egypt (comp. 51 9; Pss. 87 4 89 10; Ezek. 29 3. 4); but the Egyptian *Roar-and-rage* will prove in fact a *Sitting-still!* Blustering words end in futile deeds. The subsequent taunt of the Rabshakeh flung to Hezekiah's officers on the walls of Jerusalem, revealed the folly of their present action: "On whom dost thou trust, that thou rebellest against me?" cries the Assyrian;

is probably unauthentic and originated in a marginal gloss. It interrupts the connexion here. It is framed in imitation of the titles of chs. 13–23 (see p. 58).

"Behold, thou trustest upon the staff of this cracked reed, even upon Egypt; on which if a man lean, it will go into his hand and pierce it! So is Pharaoh king of Egypt to all that rely upon him" (36 5. 6). This exactly accords with the inscription of Sargon referring to the anti-Assyrian coalition of 711 (see pp. 77-84): "The people of Philistia, Judah, Edom, and Moab were speaking treason. The people and their evil chiefs (comp. 28 14. 15 30 4), seeking to fight against me, sent their presents unto Pharaoh, king of Egypt, a monarch who would not save them, and besought his alliance." The hollowness of Egyptian promises by this time had become proverbial; for thirty years, despite her political weakness (see pp. 12-14), she had been persistently weaving her web of intrigue and egging on the little states of Aram and Canaan to resist the great eastern power, only to betray them at the crucial moment; but experience was lost on the infatuated Judæans.

Jehovah's protest against the Egyptian treaty is to be solemnly registered by way of witness to future times: "Now go, write it on a tablet and inscribe it on a scroll, that it may serve for the future, to be a witness for ever" (comp. 8 1. 16-18). Oral prophecy takes written shape in Isaiah's age, which treasured the record of

Amos' and Hosea's ministry against Northern Israel (comp. Vol. I, pp. 81–85), and gathered the nucleus of the prophetic Scriptures. Isaiah has drawn around him a band of disciples (comp. 8 16), who will guard the deposit of his rejected word—such a one was probably the first editor of this Third Book of his (see p. 98 above); to their care we owe the preservation of his writings along with the earlier literary monuments of Israel, which survived the persecution of Manasseh and were carried by the faithful few into the Babylonian Exile, where they became the anchor of the national existence.

It is a crushing indictment that Isaiah frames in this chapter. The political leaders of his country are guilty of treason against the theocratic constitution: they are rebels toward Jehovah (ver. 9); they have striven to suppress or pervert Divine prophecy (10. 11); their power rests on oppression and trickery (12); and they are bringing on the nation swift and crushing disaster (13. 14). Had Judah but held aloof from the commotion stirred up by Egypt, in which that indolent power plays so ignoble a part, all might have been well: "Thus said the Holy One of Israel, In turning back [from this self-chosen way], and settling down, you will be saved; in keeping quiet and in trusting [Jehovah] your strength will lie" (15). But no! they will have *war*; and war they shall have, to their discomfiture (16). Meanwhile Jehovah " will wait," until "judgement" has done its work upon His people and it is time for grace to interpose; then the believing remnant will be "blessed, who wait for Him" (18).

The last clause of ver. 18 supplies the peg on which hangs the Messianic prophecy of vv. 19-26. This paragraph broadly describes the happiness of Israel in the latter days, following the storm of judgement now impending. The prediction stands in no strict connexion with the previous threatening; it may have been delivered to Isaiah's disciples at any time during this period of alarm. The coming glory of Israel will consist (*a*) in its "dwelling in Zion" at peace with Jehovah (19); (*b*) in abundance of God-given "teachers," whose word will be followed (20. 21)— this is imagined by Dr Cheyne and others to be a post-exilic, or even Rabbinical, feature of the description, but it is strictly germane to Isaiah's experience (see vv. 9-12); (*c*) idolatrous objects are to be thrown away as filthy things (22); (*d*) agriculture will richly prosper by the blessing of God (23. 24 : a favourite promise with Isaiah); and (*e*) the natural forces of life will be multiplied in the day of God's favour to His pardoned people (25. 26). Nothing is said of the Messianic *king*; but the blessings of His *kingdom* shine in their brightest colours. The complexion of the passage is Isaianic throughout, though a word here or there may suggest that it has been touched up by some editorial hand.

Vv. 27-33 are a companion picture to the former—an *Inferno* matching the *Paradiso* of 19-26. This terrible outburst of Jehovah's anger against "the Assyrian" (31) recalls the great denunciation of ch. 10 (comp. pp. 48, 52, also Vol. I, pp. 242-244). To no later epoch than that of the Assyrian devastation, and to no other writer than Isaiah, can this passionate and powerful doom-oracle be ascribed. Its sublimity of tone and force of imagination signalize it as amongst the grandest of the prophet's utterances. The image developed in the poem is that of *a funeral pyre* heaped high in the sight of the world (33), upon which the Assyrian is flung, after he has been slain by Jehovah in thunder-strokes of battle (30-32). The pile is fired by the Lord's hot wrath and fanned by His mighty breath (27. 28. 33); while, for music, both battle and funeral will be accompanied by Israel's festal songs, by strains of the flute and timbrel as on a night of holy solemnity (29. 32); comp., for this last trait, ch. 14 7.

4. *Jehovah Himself, not Egypt, Zion's protector*, chap. 31 1–32 8.—The concise prophecy of ch. 31 brings to a sharper point the issue of ch. 30, and throws into bold relief Jehovah's part in the rescue of His city and people. In vv. 1-3 the worthlessness of Egyptian help, and the offence, sorely to be punished, that is given to Jehovah by those who seek it, are stated over again; but the prophet further reveals, under the figure of a "lion growling over his prey," *Jehovah* ready to be Himself the champion of Mount Zion in her straits (4. 5); he calls on the people, in expectation of this succour, to "turn to Him, from whom the whole house of Israel [Judah no less than Ephraim] have deeply revolted," while they cast away their idols (6. 7). They shall then witness the destruction of the Assyrian, who will be overthrown by no human hand, but by "Jehovah, whose fire is in Zion and His furnace in Jerusalem" (s. 9; comp. 30 33, and 29 1—*Ariel*, i.e. *God's hearth*). The friendlier tone of this oracle bespeaks a date somewhat later than that of the foregoing chapter; reproof and threatening on Jehovah's part change increasingly into encouragement, as the Egyptian policy breaks down and the position of the city becomes, humanly speaking, more desperate. The popular feeling had, doubtless, grown subdued,

while the levity displayed in the early period of the war (22 12-14, see pp. 63-65 above) passed into dejection, not unmixed with shame and compunction; of this change we find symptoms in 30 19 31 6 32 2 33 14. 24.

Ch. 32 1-8, by the general admission of critics, forms a pendant to 31, and stands related thereto much as 30 19-26 to vv. 1-18. This is the third picture of the Messianic times we find in the Book (chs. 28–33)—the fourth if 28 16 be counted, which was an isolated image rather than a picture. The ideal blessedness of Zion grows upon Isaiah's view and fills his evening sky, being seen as about to ensue upon the defeat of the Assyrians. Manifestly it was not for this great prophet "to know times or seasons." He was granted a true vision of the glory following his people's sufferings; its *distance* his eye could not measure. While ch. 30 19-26 set forth the happy state of the coming kingdom, starting from the thought of "the people dwelling in Zion" and with the tears wiped from their face, this prediction seats the "king" in the midst of redeemed Jerusalem, "reigning in righteousness" with the circle of his "princes" about him "ruling in judgement" (ver. 1); he towers above them like a sheltering "rock," at whose foot "rivers of water" flow forth (2). The image idealizes the royal court of

Hezekiah; the coming king of Zion will have the strength and stedfastness in which the actual king has been wanting, and his "princes" will present a happy contrast to the men with whom Isaiah has had so bitter a struggle (see 28 14, etc.): this representation of the prophetic kingship may be combined with those given in 9 6, 11 1-5, and Micah 5 2-5. Common to chs. 30 and 32 is the thought of *adequate religious teaching* (vv. 3. 4; comp. 30 20. 21; also Jer. 31 34, which looks farther still)—the lack of this amongst his people Isaiah had painfully felt; and of *a lofty moral standard* (5-8), which is to be evidenced, according to this passage, in a right appreciation of the generous and gentle qualities of character. The popularity of the "fools" and "knaves" who had been of late hurrying their country to ruin, filled Isaiah with disgust; this sentiment prompts the description indirectly given in the striking verses before us, of the genuine princely nature, of the sort of men who form a true nobility, and impress on their people a sound moral taste. We decline, therefore, to follow the critics who regard vv. 6-8, along with 28 23-29, as a bit of post-Isaianic *Chokmah*, or Gnomic writing, because of its sententious, moralizing style; comp. p. 106 above.

5. *Reproof of the careless women of Jerusalem,*

chap. 32 9-20.—In what relation vv. 9-20 stand to the context it is difficult to say; and within the paragraph itself the connexion of vv. 16-20 with the rebuke of the women is far from clear. It seems best to treat this as a detached Isaianic prophecy, which has been inserted here *à propos* of the crisis of 705-701. Vv. 10-14 resemble Isaiah's earlier strain (see 6 11. 12 5 5. 6. 9. 10, etc., 7 21-25), rather than that of the Third Book, in the continued desolation of the land and ruin of the city which they foretell; the scourge of Sennacherib's invasion, when it came, the prophet expected to be speedily removed, leaving Mount Zion unviolated (see 29 5-8 30 31 31 4-9 33 17-21). The stern, contemptuous threatening addressed to the "careless women," the "heedless daughters" of Jerusalem, in vv. 9-12 is quite in the vein of ch. 3 16-4 1 (comp. Amos 6 1), and was first uttered, probably, about the same time (see pp. 34-35); thirty years later it is still sadly appropriate. With sure insight Isaiah traces the moral decay and apostasy of the Judæan state to the luxury and frivolity of its fashionable ladies, a chief spring of mischief to society. The reckless, self-indulgent women of vv. 9-11 were the mothers or wives of the "fools" and the "churls" above described in vv. 5-8, and were largely responsible for their being such; they are going to be punished accordingly. Such a connexion holds good, in the nature of things, between the second and first halves of ch. 32. The whole country and city will share in the punishment designed for their "heedless daughters" (vv. 13. 14); forsaken palaces and ravaged fields will bear witness to the crimes of a heartless, godless womanhood.

Vv. 15-20 introduce the Messianic hope to relieve the utter gloom of the future just described. These sentences predict an effusion of Jehovah's "spirit from on high" (15), producing a transformation in all existing conditions of life (just as in 29 17); this will lead to the establishment of justice and peace (17. 18), on the downfall of the foreign oppressor (19 ; comp. 10 33. 34), and to the restoring of a happy rural life (20 ; comp. 30 23. 24). The oracle is, however, brought in so abruptly and with so little apparent reference to the previous threatening, that it is naturally regarded as a fragment coming from some other context, which has been inserted here as an offset to the terrible conclusion of vv. 9-14, and in order to maintain the balancing of mercy against judgement which characterizes the Book throughout. The idyllic little picture of the Messianic felicity —a mere *peep* into the future—is from Isaiah's artist hand. Ver. 19, however, seems disturbing and out of place; this may be set down as a marginal gloss. The promise of the "outpouring of the Spirit" (15) recalls Joel's memorable prophecy (2 28. 29; see Vol. I, pp. 113-115; and comp. Isa. 11 2), which is re-echoed and enlarged subsequently in ch. 44 3 and Ezek. 36 26. 27.

6. *Assyrian treachery and the vindication of Zion*, chap. 33.—This chapter is continuous with the last in time and contents; it reveals the same poise of punishment and pardon—the secret of Jerusalem's coming redemption through suffering —which governs the construction of chs. 28-32. The occasion of the "Woe" upon Assyria (ver. 1) is supplied by 2 Kings 18 13-17: Sennacherib, when he invaded Palestine to suppress the revolt instigated by Egypt, had at first accepted Hezekiah's submission and the heavy fine which he paid in acknowledgement of his offence; no sooner had he done this than he sent a force to demand the unconditional surrender of the city. By such action the Assyrian king put himself completely in the wrong; so that, from this point onwards, Isaiah promises to his compatriots Jehovah's protection in the most unqualified sense. "The ambassadors of peace," in ver. 7, are the Judæan negotiators, returning deceived and flouted from the enemy's camp; comp. the scene of 36 22. Ver. 9 depicts the devastation,

complete and systematic, inflicted on the Israelite country by the Assyrians—an injury from which Palestine has probably never quite recovered. By a sudden turn of language, vv. 10-12 hurl against the invaders the threat of Jehovah's swift retribution (ver. 11 is addressed to *the enemy*); the time has come at last for Israel's God to interfere :

Now will I arise, saith Jehovah :
Now will I lift up Myself; now will I be exalted !
Ye shall bring forth chaff; ye shall conceive stubble :
Your snorting—it is a fire that will devour yourselves !
And the peoples shall be as lime-burnings,
As thorns cut down, that in the fire are consumed !

Ver. 11 presupposes the vengeance as already exacted, and God's city delivered by a stroke of judgement so astounding that it makes "the sinners in Zion affrighted" (14), while it assures safety and sustenance to the faithful (15. 16). "The king" will once more wear his robes of "beauty" (contrast 37 1 ; and comp. 52 1); and Zion, after the straitness of her siege, will look out over "far-stretching" provinces, from which the foreign exactor has disappeared, leaving "Jerusalem a quiet habitation, a tent that shall not be removed" (17-20). "In place of the broad rivers and streams" (the advantage which Jerusalem signally lacked, as compared with other capitals)

"Jehovah" Himself—or, as some critics would emend the text, "the brook of Jehovah," *i.e.* Siloam (comp. the contemporary Psalm 46 4, etc.)—will be there, for His people's defence and refreshment (21. 22). The disabled ship of state, now labouring in the tempest, shall yet reach its port (23). Sickness of body, with distress of mind, will be unknown in the redeemed community (24). The four concluding verses have added new features to the prophetic delineation of God's perfected kingdom in Israel; comp. 30 19-26, 32 1-8.

This sixth section forms a delightful and fitting close to the cycle of Isaiah's prophecies now reviewed; there is scarcely anything in its contents that we need be surprised to find proceeding from him. Now at length, in the climax of the struggle and in the agony of Jerusalem's shame and terror, Jehovah's rebukes give place wholly to comfort and promise, and "mercy," as never before, "rejoices over against judgement." At the same time, certain difficulties attach to the authorship of the chapter. "The march, force, fulness, and flow of Isaiah's speech are missed here," says Kittel; and there are many locutions in it otherwise strange to his writings—one Hebrew particle even occurring six times in vv. 20-24, without any clear necessity, which

Isaiah never uses elsewhere; the composition is lyrical instead of oratorical, and runs into short elliptical sentences and disconnected figures, in a way foreign to Isaiah's well-marked style. Some have found in the excitement of the prophet at this crisis an explanation of the hurried and broken manner of discourse. Dr Cheyne, in his *Commentary*, ed. 3 explained the altered style by conjecturing that " Isaiah left this prophecy imperfectly prepared for publication "—in more recent discussions he ascribes the chapter, like much besides formerly vindicated for Isaiah, to quite a late period of Israelite prophecy. Dillmann suggested that the discourse is from the pen of a reporter of Isaiah's speech; Ewald, that some prophetic disciple of Isaiah wrote it (comp. 8 16); Kittel thinks that a genuine oracle of Isaiah's has here been rewritten and expanded by a post-exilic author, who makes allusions to Pss. 15, 24, 46, and 48. One feels that the general scope, temper, and atmosphere of the chapter are Isaianic, and many touches of thought and language remind us of the master; while there are other expressions which, in keeping with the structure and movement of the paragraphs, incline us to recognise the working of another but a sympathetic mind, imbued with Isaiah's ideas and belonging to his age and school. Dillmann's or Ewald's theory, as stated above, appears to us best to suit the facts. The parallels with the Book of Psalms adduced by Kittel are insufficient ground for crediting the chapter to a post-exilic writer. The image presented of the ideal Zion and its territory is itself consistent, and such as would naturally take shape at the time of the war with Sennacherib.

Chs. 34 and 35 supplement Book III of Isaiah and form a finalé to it, in the same sense in which chs. 24-27 supplement 13-23 (see pp. 94-96 above); they give to the foregoing collection of oracles a wider scope, and apply their conception of redemption for Israel through chastening and judgement on her foes to the altered world of exilic and post-exilic times. Ch. 35 is a joyous appeal, couched in lyrical strain, to the banished sons of Zion, which assures them that the way is open, and bids them cross the desert without fear under Jehovah's conduct. The Babylonian captivity is presupposed as matter of past history—so Delitzsch, who had previously defended the Isaianic authorship, came to admit in the last (fourth) edition of his *Commentary*. The graphic description of the wilderness journey seems to imply experience of it on the poet's own part; one may best read the message as an invitation from some gifted spokesman of the Return urging his brethren still in exile to take courage themselves also to come home. There are clear echoes of Isaiah 40 in this inspired writer, as well as of ch. 32 above; see the Revised marginal references.

But ch. 35, with its enchanting promises, has its background in ch. 34, which comes from the same author's hand. The latter prophecy begins as a wholesale denunciation (ver. 1; comp. 24 1) of Jehovah's fierce anger, as yet unsatisfied, upon the peoples who have used Israel so cruelly (ver. 2; comp. Zech. 1 14. 15. 21):

Draw near, ye nations, to hear; and ye peoples, hearken!
Let the earth hear, and its fulness,—the world, and all things that come forth of it!
For Jehovah hath a wrath against all the nations, and a hot anger against all the host of them:
He hath put them under the ban; He hath given them up to slaughter!

Thus a storm of judgement, of an appalling violence, is to sweep over the earth universally (3. 4; comp. 24 1-15). This cosmopolitan survey and the wide outlook upon God's dealings with nations which chs. 24 and 34 reveal, are due to the experiences of the Exile and to the involvement of Israel's fate in that of the world-empires ensuing therefrom. The seer of Israel who thus writes, has looked out on the affairs of mankind from some imperial centre, such as Babylon; yet the passions of Jewish nationality burn in his breast. For it is on *Edom* that he sees Jehovah's vengeance about to fall in its uttermost force (5-17); on this prospect he dilates, for the rest of the chapter, with a relish resembling that of Psalm 137 and characteristic of the literature of this period (comp. ch. 63; Jer. 49 7-22; Lam. 4 21. 22; Ezek. 25 8-17; contrast with these the milder tone of Isa. 21 11. 12, and of the Book of Obadiah—see Vol. I, pp. 85 ff.), which fastens upon Edom as the object of Israel's fiercest resentment. This people of kindred blood had taken a conspicuous part in the humiliation of Judah, and showed a malignant delight, which the Jews have never forgotten, at the destruction of Jerusalem.

The Historical Appendix, contained in chs. 36-39, has been extracted from the 2nd Book of Kings, like ch. 52 concluding the prophecies of Jeremiah. The *Prayer of Hezekiah,* inserted in ch. 38 (9-20)—a psalm and not a prophecy—is, however, wanting in Kings. The reference to the death of Sennacherib (681 B.C.) which is made in 37 38, indicates that the narrative is post-Isaianic in its composition, and it refers to the prophet throughout in the third person. The story of the siege of Jerusalem bears every sign of historicity. The attitude and language of Isaiah as here reported, and the relations in which he appears toward king and people, are in keeping with what we find in his previous oracles. Book III of the prophecies (chs. 28-33) leads up to the triumph of Isaiah, which chs. 36 and 37 so powerfully describe. The deliverance of Jerusalem at the hour of extreme peril, and the destruction of the Assyrian host, were the crown and the vindication of Isaiah's entire ministry. He has reached the summit of his strenuous and lofty career, and thus passes from the stage of the sacred history. For observations on the matter of these four chapters, see pp. 15-20, and 120 above.

CHAPTER XVII

THE MESSIANIC TEACHING OF ISAIAH

The Messianic King and Kingdom — The Davidic Monarchy—Failure of the Historical Kingship—Enlargement of the Kingdom—Effect of Assyrian Rule on the Messianic Ideal—National Framework of the Messiahship—Cleansing of the Actual Zion—The Ideal King to match the Ideal City and Kingdom—The Boy Immanuel—The Prince of the Four Names—A True King the Need of the Times—The Birth-hour of Messianic Prophecy—Retreat of the Messianic Idea—Defects of Isaiah's Doctrine.

THE Messianic doctrine of the Old Testament, in its wider sense, embraces the conception of the ideal kingdom of God along with that of the ideal king. The second of these notions arose historically out of the former, and cannot be understood apart from it. In Isaiah's mind and teaching this development of the spirit of prophecy found its chief instrument, and the volume of Isaiah became the great text-book of Old Testament Messianism. The *kingdom* this prophet is always thinking of; the coming *king* is the subject of special and detached oracles, and emerged at a particular crisis in his ministry. But though the passages describing the Messiah-king are few in number and brief in extent (chs. 9 6.7 and 11 1-5; the inclusion of 7 14-16 and 8 8 in this list is questionable, as will afterwards appear), they occupy a salient position in Isaiah's life-work; they signalize a critical epoch in the growth of his own ideas, and in the unfolding of the purposes of God concerning Israel. Isa. 9 6.7 and 11 1-5 stand close together as amongst the summits of Old Testament thought, points at which the genius of Israel reached its loftiest flight and took its farthest view into the future.[1]

The Israelite constitution was fundamentally theocratic, admitting in its original form of no earthly monarch; a revolution was accomplished under the prophet Samuel, which met with decided resistance and took effect only by degrees, when the throne of David was established and a sacrosanct character was conferred upon his line. Henceforth the Divine rule was impersonated in the reigning son of David; but his administration tended more often than not to

---

[1] The school of German critics with which Dr Cheyne associates himself, attempt to cut out these great passages, and all other strictly Messianic references, from the Isaianic context. See pp. 28, 46, 53 above.

lower its ideal, and even threatened in the reigns of Ahaz and Manasseh its complete effacement in the minds of the people. Especially at such times the prophets were compelled to recall and meditate upon "the pattern shown" them "in the mount." They worked under two fixed presuppositions—axioms of prophecy from the date of the oracle of 2 Sam. 7—viz. the ethical perfection and integrity of Jehovah's rule in Israel, and the perpetuity of the Davidic dynasty.

The history of the Judæan monarchy showed, through one bitter experience after another, that these necessities could be reconciled only in a superhuman son of David; they demanded a prince filled with the Spirit of Jehovah and furnished with royal qualities such as no child of man had ever shown, one who should stand in a relation of nearness to God hitherto unexampled and lifting him above human frailties and limitations. As it was with the political *kingdoms* of Israel and of Judah in turn, so it proved with the historical *kings*: from the failure of the actual and the present the religious thinkers of Israel took refuge in the region of the ideal future, where the true soul of the people learnt abidingly to make its home. Isaiah "looked for the city which hath the foundations, whose builder and maker is God"; he looked at the same time for the King of that city, the perfect Prince and Son of God, who should be "set upon the throne of David, to establish it with judgement and with righteousness from henceforth even for ever" (Isa. 9 7). Otherwise God's promises will be made void; and the holy city and royal house, marvellously preserved in the general overthrow, will have been saved to no purpose. Therefore "the zeal of Jehovah of hosts will perform this."

Thus, with the calamities falling on the Israelite kingship, it took on in prophecy a nobler ideal character; at the same time, it received a wider scope. This double movement characterizes the Isaianic Messianism. Before the eyes of the prophets the Assyrian power, with portentous rapidity, had grown into a world-empire. God's people sit no longer solitary and apart with their Jehovah: their children have been dragged in thousands to distant exile; Judæa is made a fief of Nineveh. Israel is involved in the fate of other nations and in the polity of the Great Powers around her. The coming King, if he is to bring salvation for *her*, must be able to command *them*. It is no longer enough for the chosen people to "sit each man under his own vine and fig-tree" in the land of Canaan; there must be "a highway out of Egypt to Assyria" for international friendship and "Israel" must become "the third with Egypt and with Assyria, a blessing in the midst of the earth" (19 23. 24), if God's kingdom is to be securely settled amongst men. So the Messianic rule begins to assume in idea world-dimensions, and to entertain (if one may so speak) imperial ambitions. The horizon of Psalm 72 extended no further than Solomon's domains and the boundaries of Palestine and Syria: "He shall reign from sea to sea [from the Mediterranean to the Elanitic Gulf], and from the river [Euphrates] to the ends of the land" [the borders of the Southern Desert]. Far different is the prospect over which Isaiah's eye ranges, when he sees "the mountain of Jehovah's house established in the top of the mountains, and all nations flowing into it," when from Zion God "judges between the nations" and forbids them to "learn war any more," when "the root of Jesse is set for an ensign of the peoples" and "unto him the nations seek," while "the earth is filled with the knowledge of Jehovah, as the waters cover the sea" (Isa. 2 2-4 11 9. 10).

The Assyrian conquests, which enlarged the range of the Messianic vision, served in a negative sense to determine its contents. The nature and aims and methods of a true world-sovereignty came to be defined by their contraries. Rarely have invasions been more savage and destructive, never have subject populations been treated more inhumanly than were the provinces under the rule of Asshur. The kings of Nineveh combined with vast ambitions and military genius an utter disregard of justice and ignorance of the principles of good government. Hence rebellions occurred at each opportunity, in almost every quarter of the empire, and the west of Asia was kept in a fever of war. *Righteousness* and *peace* are therefore, in Isaiah's aspirations, the great desiderata of the times; *faithfulness, gentleness,* and *wisdom* clothe the Messianic ruler whom he portrays. He dreams of an idyllic state wherein the beasts of prey, which men have learnt to copy, lay aside their fierceness; the fangs of the wolf and the poison of the asp forget their use; swords are fashioned into ploughshares, spears into pruning-hooks (2_4 9_{4-7} 11_{1-9}). To this paradise of the coming age Isaiah's spirit fled from the wasted cities and ravaged lands and corpse-strewn fields of battle, that met his gaze on all sides. The passionate hatred and lofty scorn that breathe in his denunciation of the Assyrian power in chap. 10 supply the prelude and the dark background to his idealization of the true

King of men in the exquisite lines of chap. 11. Isaiah, first of the prophets, grasps and unfolds the sublime conception, latent in previous revelations, of a universal ethical kingdom of God extending over all nature with mankind, which will have its metropolis in mount Zion and its ruler, God's true and worthy vicegerent, in the perfect Son of David.

This grand enlargement of the Messianic dominion in no way compromises its relations to Israel; Isaiah holds fast to the national form and framework of the Covenant. Indeed, when the nation had been reduced by the loss of the Ten Tribes and Israel became synonymous with Judah, the regard of prophecy was concentrated more and more upon Jerusalem and the throne of David. The *people* and the *city* are identified in Isaiah's thoughts. "The redemption of Jerusalem" becomes his absorbing solicitude. The "inhabitants of Jerusalem and the men of Judah" form the community to which Jehovah makes appeal; they are "the plant of His delight" (5 1-7). In the Sennacherib crisis the whole fate and future of the covenant-people turn upon the deliverance of Mount Zion. The blessedness of the coming times is to be realized, specifically, in the moral transformation of Jerusalem: when through the scattering of the besieging heathen Zion has become "a quiet habitation, a tent that shall not be removed," and when she can be "called the city of righteousness, the faithful city," since "Jehovah has washed away the filth of the daughters of Zion and has purged the blood of Jerusalem from the midst thereof" (see 1 $_{26}$ 4 $_{4-6}$ 32 $_{5, 6}$ 33 $_{20-24}$), the millennium will have arrived; then "the law will go forth out of Zion, and the word of Jehovah from Jerusalem" (2 $_3$), to fill the world with righteousness and truth. This is the consummation of the kingdom of God, for Israel and the nations, as Isaiah imagined it. But first Zion herself—who is "Ariel" (the hearth of God)—shall be cleansed "by the spirit of judgement and the spirit of burning"; so purified, she will serve as "Jehovah's furnace" to consume the pride and glory of Asshur; or (to change the figure) the rock of "foundation" is "laid in Zion" on which the hostile nations "shall be broken in pieces" and the Assyrian power for ever shattered (4 $_4$ 8 14 $_{25}$ 28 $_{16}$ 29 $_1$ 30 $_{27-33}$ 31 $_9$).

The world-kingdom of Jehovah is thus focussed at Jerusalem; the Mighty One of Israel, the God of the whole earth, is worshipped as "Jehovah of hosts which dwelleth in Mount Zion" (8 $_{18}$). This merging of the land in the city, the centring of all the interests of God's kingdom, moral and material, in one sacred spot, is deeply characteristic of the personal genius and situation of Isaiah, and of the epoch of revelation of which he was the exponent. The contest between God's kingdom and the evil powers of the world has taken a shape in which Jehovah's honour, the preservation of His name and faith, is bound up with the safety of a single city—a place which in its existing condition, and judged by its own deserts, is morally indefensible! "I will defend this city to save it for Mine own sake, and for My servant David's sake"; such was Jehovah's word of defiance to Sennacherib pronounced through Isaiah (37 35).

For Jerusalem and her citizens as they are, Isaiah anticipates nothing but suffering and shame. The vision that filled his imagination and guided his policy through forty years of patient struggle with weak or traitorous kings and vain worldly-wise counsellors, is that of a holy city with its filth consumed in the flames of judgement, tenanted by a righteous and happy people, obedient to their God, kindly and faithful towards each other. Through the lurid fires of the Assyrian conflict he saw the coming of the city of God; he counts upon it that Zion will emerge from this trial delivered not only from her secular foe, but from the sins that had wrought her debasement.

Now the ideal *king* of Isaiah's visions is the counterpart of the ideal city and kingdom he is looking and working for. The latter, under the given historical situation, implies the former. The new Jerusalem and the sanctified Israel of the future could not be conceived apart from their *redeemer*, the God-given deliverer and ruler, who from his throne in Zion will extend the blessings of righteousness and peace, along with the knowledge of Jehovah, over all surrounding peoples and to the ends of the earth. His person and his rule are set forth in terms that pass far beyond the limits of human infirmity and change; he is clothed with the majesty of the God he represents, who executes through His "son" His gracious designs toward His people and all peoples. Accordingly, the coming king is adumbrated first in the sign of "Immanuel" (*With-us-is-God*, or *-the-Mighty-One*), that was addressed to the distrustful and half-apostate Ahaz (7 10-17). The boy to whom the prophet gives, before his conception, this exalted and reassuring name is the child of some unknown "damsel." There is nothing to indicate the mother's connexion with the Davidic house: it may be that fear of Ahaz's jealousy made the reference designedly vague. But his birth under this title, at this crisis, supplies, to all who are in the secret, a pledge of the presence of Israel's God and the safety of His land. "Immanu-el" will be reared on the produce of fields from which tillage has ceased (ver. 15); but before he reaches years of understanding, the forces of Damascus and Samaria, at the moment overpowering Judah, will be shattered (16).

So far, indeed, there is no hint of any royal character being ascribed to the boy Immanuel personally; his significance—as in the case of Isaiah's own sons (7 3 8 3. 18)—lies in his *name*, and in the conditions under which his infancy will be spent. But when, at a later date and subsequently to the child's birth (see pp. 41–45 above), the prophet speaks of the Assyrian flood as "filling the breadth of *thy land*, O 'Immanu-el'" (8 8), it looks as though Judæa belonged to the boy in question and he were thought of as the destined heir of David's throne. Some, therefore, have identified Immanuel with *Hezekiah*, Ahaz's successor; but chronology forbids this. If the little Immanuel were some other scion of the royal house whose enthronement Isaiah expected, it is strange that nothing more is heard about him and that the prophet, as would appear, acquiesced in his dropping into obscurity. It is safer to suppose, with Kittel,[1] that Judæa is called "Immanu-el's land" as the native land of the boy who bears this glorious name; and that the child is thus distinguished not at all in virtue of his affinity to the ruling house, but as "the representative of the new generation of Judæans" and as standing for those who believe that "God is with us," the true Israel to whom God's salvation is pledged despite the troubles now overwhelming the country. The New Testament fulfilment gave to this watchword of Isaiah an import incomparably loftier than that in which the prophet conceived it, but in essential consistency with his meaning (see Matt. 1 23).

While the name "Immanu-el," conferred on a child of Israel by God's direction, was a pledge of the Almighty Presence guarding Jehovah's land, the prophecy of ch. 9 6 points to that Presence as it will be one day disclosed in the advent of the true king of men, that child of God's people through whom its divine character and office will at length be realized: "A child is born to us, a son is given to us; and the government shall be upon his shoulder."

---

[1] See his *Der Prophet Yesaja*, Kurtzgef. exeg. Handbuch zum A.T.³, *ad loc.*

Another birth is thus foretold, and this time in the royal succession. But the prophet thinks of the coming one as the child of the nation more than of the Davidic house—" born *to us*" (so Jesus styled Himself "Son of man," not Son of David); for he will impersonate and express the genius of Israel itself, and will lift his race with him to the height of their calling. To this great heir of the national destiny an unexampled designation is given; he is *the Prince of the Four Names*: "Wonder of a counsellor, God of a hero, Father for evermore, Prince of peace." In Isaiah's description the idea of the Messiah-king with which revelation has been charged ever since the age of Samuel precipitates itself, under the shock of the Assyrian crisis; the labour of prophecy for the last three hundred years comes to birth. There are no marks of time attached to the prediction, such as were necessary in the case of the boy Immanuel; only Isaiah knows that such a glorious ruler must and will be born for God's people. That he will issue from David's family goes without saying. The throne founded by God in Zion (28 16) he will redeem from the humiliation it is suffering (2 11-17 3 14 7 17); and ch. 11 $^{1-5}$ resumes the description of the character and administration of the coming Prince, signifying that he will appear as "a shoot from the stock [*or* stump] of Jesse, and a sprout from his roots" (comp. Mic. 5 3; and Vol. I, p. 260). The predictions of chs. 9 and 11 are assigned to the period about the end of Ahaz's and the beginning of Hezekiah's reign, when the honour of the crown was at its lowest and the dynasty was like a tree cut down to the stump (comp. Amos 9 11). A miraculous revival is thus promised for the empire of David, to be realised in the person of a future king of godlike attributes—a new and nobler Solomon, since he is called Prince of Peace—who will raise his people to unexampled happiness and extend his sway widely through the world and over the domain of nature, a sovereign whose kingdom appears to know no bounds either of space or time. Ch. 9 6, 7 throws emphasis on the wisdom, power, and grandeur of the destined prince and the durability of his rule; ch. 11 1-5 brings out his religious character: he will be endued with the sevenfold spirit of Jehovah; and his administration will be discerning and gracious, bringing defence to the poor and lowly and ruin on their wicked oppressors.

The times in which Isaiah lived demanded above everything strong, wise, and God-fearing rulers. "A king shall reign in righteousness, and princes shall rule in judgement" (32 1. 2) : this was the one hope of society. "*A man*" is needed, who should be "as an hiding-place from the wind and a covert from the tempest; as rivers of water in a dry place, and the shadow of a great rock in a weary land." Monarchy is the universal form of national existence; the disposition and ability of the ruler constitute the chief factor in the public well-being, alike for the little principalities of Palestine and the great empires of Egypt and Assyria. By the end of the disastrous reign of Ahaz and before the middle of his prophetic career, Isaiah had come to the conviction that through this means the salvation of Israel must be won. He had learnt how much an evil king could do to corrupt and betray the people; he had seen the Assyrian monarchy made a frightful scourge for its neighbours in the west. Jehovah, he is thereby taught and inspired to believe, will raise up in Zion a king who shall be in kingly character and in the beneficence of his rule the precise opposite of these examples, whose sway shall be wider and mightier than that of Nineveh, and whose justice and compassion will exceed those of the best princes of David's historic line. The promise originally made to David thus transforms itself, and comes to signify no longer the indefinite perpetuity of the reigning house, but the perfection of kingship that is to be realized in the prince who is its consummate issue.

The conception of the Messianic royalty is the genuine offspring of the epoch of Isaiah, and forms its chief contribution to the course of history. As Kittel says,[1] "The hour in which Isaiah parted from Ahaz gave to the world the thought of the Messiah." Henceforth this idea becomes a fixed datum in the religious life of Israel; it was born in the soul of this kingliest of the prophets. The basis of the expectation lay in the covenant promise made to David (2 Sam. 7); the material out of which it was shaped to its existing form was supplied by the Assyrian-Judaean crisis of the eighth century. The time was ripe for its production, and its origination cannot, with any fair probability, be referred to a later age or situation than that of Isaiah of Jerusalem, as he confronted Ahaz on the one side and the Assyrian despotism on the other; nor can it be credited to a prophet of lesser genius and weaker character than Isaiah possessed.

It is true that under Hezekiah, and in the later stage of Isaiah's teaching, the image of the Messiah king retreats from view; the prophet descends from the ideal heights of chs. 9 and 11.

[1] *History of the Hebrews*, vol. ii, p. 346.

Nor is this to be wondered at. Isaiah's attention was again engaged by the more immediate future; the deliverance of the city and the reformation of the people become his absorbing interests. Hezekiah, though vacillating and infirm, was a pious, well-intentioned prince, whose behaviour no longer, like that of his father, drove the prophet into despair of the existing monarchy. "The king" whom Jerusalem "shall see in his beauty," ruling over "a land of far distances" (33 17), need be none other than the living son of David, raised from the state of fear and disfigurement to which Hezekiah was reduced in the Assyrian siege (37 1). The 33rd chapter, which appears to contain Isaiah's latest visions "concerning Judah and Jerusalem," reveals "Jehovah" Himself "with us in majesty" (comp. the motto "Immanu-el" of chs. 7 and 8), whose enthronement there makes "Jerusalem a secure habitation"; "Jehovah is our judge, Jehovah our lawgiver, Jehovah our king," who "will save us" (vv. 20-22). Thus Isaiah reverts at the end to the fundamental thought of the theocracy, viz. that Jehovah, and no other, reigns in Israel. In God's eternal glory the Messianic sovereignty disappears, even as St Paul conceived the mediatorial reign of Jesus to be consummated by His "delivering up the kingdom to

God the Father, that God may be all in all" (1 Cor. 15 24-28).

From the above sketch of Isaiah's Messianic views it will be seen how great a step forward prophecy takes in him toward the Christian fulfilment, and yet how far remote the prophetic ideal still remained, in its form of imagination and in its material contents, from the reality finally presented in the person and work of the incarnate Son of God. Seven hundred years of suffering and change must elapse before the vision of the Son of David takes shape in Jesus Christ. More distinctly than any earlier seer, Isaiah "saw His glory and spake of Him"; he apprehended the royalty of character belonging to the world's Redeemer, and the intimate relations to God in which He must stand. Isaiah predicts in clearer outline and stronger colours than any of his fellows the largeness of the Messiah's empire, the graciousness of His government, and the happiness it brings to men. His prophecies to this effect are even now in course of fulfilment, as the kingdom of Christ extends amongst the nations and gains a completer dominance in human life.

But the Isaiah of this period knew nothing of the sufferings by which "the Christ" was to "enter into His glory," nor of His atoning sacrifice for the transgressions of mankind. That knowledge was reserved for his great pupil and successor of the sixth century (Isa. 52, 53), and for the people of the Exile. A prolonged and severe discipline was required that Israel might learn *how* the true Deliverer of men claims to rule, not by right of royal blood but by self-effacing service. The image of the warrior Messiah gives place to that of the despised and suffering " servant of Jehovah." Burdened with the guilt and shame of His fellows, by the bearing of this load—not by " striking through kings in the day of his wrath " and " filling the battle-field with dead bodies "—He shall win from God His people's restoration, and for Himself a Divine honour and a grateful and universal obedience such as accrue to no other sovereignty. Suffering and humiliation in abundance Isaiah foresees; but in the shape of chastisement falling on the sinful people itself—a dispensation of judgement out of which Israel, as the prophet hopes, will emerge morally renewed, and prepared to receive its true king and to fulfil its part as the " kingdom of priests " amongst the nations of the earth. How vain these expectations of the patriot prophet were, so far as they concerned the nearer future, Manasseh's reign was speedily to prove.

ANALYSIS OF ISAIAH 1-39.

	Chapter.	Date B.C.
I. THE EARLIER PROPHECIES: Isaiah's First Book (put together by himself); on Israel's False and True Glory	1-11[12]	c. 740-720
1. Preface: *The Great Arraignment*	1	734 (?)
2. *Vindication of the Holy One upon His People*	2-5, with 9 8-10 4	
(1) Discourses on the Cleansing Judgement, gathered from the preaching of Jotham's reign	2-4	
(2) Poems of the Coming Judgement	5, 9 8-10 4	740-735
(a) The Love-song of Jehovah's Vineyard	5 1-7	
(b) The Rhapsody of the Seven Woes and the Unslaked Anger	5 8-25, with 9 8-10 4	
(c) The Vision of the Invaders	5 26-30	
3. *Encounter with Ahaz, and Consequent Oracles*	6 1-9 7	734
(1) The Preface, relating Isaiah's Call	6	740 (original date)
(2) Story of Meeting of King and Prophet	7	
(a) Promised Defeat of Rezin and Pekah	vv. 1-9	
(b) The "Immanu-el" token given and expounded	10-17	
(c) Four Warnings concerning "that day"	18-24	
(3) Signs of the Impending Judgement	8	
(a) Name of Prophet's Son	vv. 1-4	734
(b) The Euphrates Flood	5-8	
(c) Israel's Rock a Stumbling-block	9-15	
(d) The Hiding of Jehovah's Face	16-18	
(e) Necromancy the Path of Death	19-22	
(4) Light beyond Night; the Child-prince of the Four Names	9 1-7	

ANALYSIS OF ISAIAH 1-39

	Chapter.	Date B.C.
4 *Ruin of the Assyrian, Rise of the Messianic Empire*	10 5–11 16	722–720 (?)
(1) Jehovah's Vengeance on the King of Assyria	10 5-34	
(*a*) The Axe that flouts its Wielder	vv. 5-15	
(*b*) Assyria's Punishment, Zion's Redemption	16-27	
(*c*) The Invader's Swift Approach, and Sudden Overthrow	28-34	
(2) The Rule of Jesse's Scion	11	
(*a*) His Wise, Upright, Faithful Spirit	vv. 2-5	
(*b*) His Peaceful Realm	6-10	
(*c*) The Return of Jehovah's Exiles	11-16	
Chh. 2-5 probably formed the nucleus of the above, published in 734, and enlarged by the introduction and sequel about the year 721.		
[5. *Concluding Hymn of Praise*	12	Of late origin]
II. SECOND BOOK, (CHIEFLY) OF DOOMS ON THE FOREIGN NATIONS: a loosely formed collection, the contents of which we have arranged above in the following order:—	13–23	
A. On Israelite Affairs:		
(1) *Against Samaria*, misentitled "the Burden of Damascus"	17 1-11	*c*. 735
(2) *Against Festive Jerusalem*	22 1-14	701 (early in the siege)
(3) *Against Shebna'*	15-25	earlier
B. Oracles against Foreign Peoples:		
(1) *Against Asshur*	14 24-27	*c*. 721 (?)
(2) *Against the Nations*	17 12-14	*c*. 701 (?)
(3) *Against Philistia*	14 28-32	727
(4) *Against Tyre* (or *Zidon*?)	23 1-14	722 (?)
[A Post-exilic Supplement	vv. 15-19	*c*. 520]

	Chapter.	Date B.C.
(5) *Against Egypt and Ethiopia*	20	*c.* 711
(6) *Against Moab*, rehearsing, with brief conclusion, an archaic Oracle	15, 16	
(7) *Against Edom:* this, like the last, seems to have a pre-Isaianic basis	21 11. 12	714–711 (?)
(8) *Against the Dedanites*	21 13-17	
(9) *Concerning Cush* (Ethiopia): not strictly hostile	18	*c.* 701 (?)
(10) *Concerning Egypt (and Asshur)*.	19	after 701 (?)
C. Post-Isaianic Oracles:		
(1) *On the Fall of Babylon*	21 1-10	*c.* 549 (?)
(2) *Pæan over Fallen Babylon*	13 2-14 23	*c.* 538 (?)]
[*First Apocalyptic Appendix*	24–27	Late Post-exilic (?)]
III. LATER PROPHECIES: Isaiah's Third Book (put together perhaps by a disciple: see §16), on Jehovah's Plan for the Future in opposition to the Judæan Politicians	28–33	701–701
Introductory, recalling an old oracle of Isaiah, on *Ephraim's Ruin*, applying its *Lesson for Zion*	28	
(*a*) "Woe to drunken Ephraim!"	vv. 1-6	*c.* 724 (original date)
(*b*) Like Woe to Jerusalem's Drunkards!	7-13	
(*c*) False Trust of Jerusalem's Scorners	14-22	704–703 (?)
(*d*) Isaiah's Apologue	23-29	
Redemption of Jerusalem through Chastisement	29	*c.* 703 (Feast of Tabernacles)
(*a*) The coming Siege; Besiegers scattered: "Woe to Ariel!"	vv. 1-8	
(*b*) Stupidity of the People	9-14	
(*c*) Purblind Cunning of the Statesmen: "Woe to those hiding their counsel from Jehovah!"	15-18	
(*d*) Illumination by Jehovah	19-21	

	Chapter.	Date B.C.
3. *Denunciation of the Treaty with Egypt* .	30	703 or 702
(*a*) This Step a Defiance of Jehovah: "Woe to the rebellious children!" .	vv. 1-5	
(*b*) Profitless Embassy across the Desert.	6, 7	
(*c*) Attempt to silence the Prophet . .	8-14	
(*d*) Rejection of the Way of Quiet Trust .	15-18	
(*e*) View of ultimate Messianic Felicity .	19-26	
(*f*) The Funeral Pyre of the Assyrian .	27-32	
4. *Jehovah, not Egypt, Zion's Protector*	31 1–32 8	702 or 701
(*a*) Futility of Egyptian Help . . .	31 1-3	
(*b*) Jehovah fighting for His People	4-9	
(*c*) Reign of the Coming King . .	32 1-8	
* * * * *		
(*d*) Reproof of the Careless Women of Jerusalem: a detached Isaianic fragment	32 9-14	(?)
* * * * *		
(*e*) Messianic Felicity—another fragment	32 15-20	*c.* 701 (?)
* * * * *		
5. *Assyrian Treachery, and the Vindication of Zion*	33	701
(*a*) "Woe to the Treacherous Dealer!" and Comfort for Zion . . .	vv. 1-6	
(*b*) Desolation of the Land, which Jehovah will avenge	7-12	
(*c*) Effect of Zion's Deliverance, and Blissful State of the Redeemed People	13-21	
Many think that ch. 33 comes, in whole or part, from some disciple of Isaiah, who in that case has probably compiled the whole Book, chs. 28–33, completing his master's teaching in his vein.		
[*Second Apocalyptic Appendix* . . .	34, 35	Post-exilic ?]
Historical Supplement to Isa. 1–35, from 2 Kings 18 13–20 19, with a slight rearrangement, and with the insertion of Hezekiah's Song. . . .	36 1–38 8 38 21–39 8 38 9-20	Kings composed in the Exile.

CHAPTER XVIII

THE REACTION UNDER MANASSEH

Passing of Isaiah's Generation—Heathen Revival in Jerusalem—Account of Manasseh's Reign in 2 Kings—Manasseh's Assyrianising Policy—Its Fatal Consequences—Reversal of Isaiah's Hopes—Tradition of Isaiah's Murder—Causes of the Manassite Revolution—Religious Syncretism and Broad Statesmanship—Testimony of Mic. 6, 7—Light shining in a Dark Place — Concealment of Deuteronomy — Nahum's Message to Judah — The Episode of 2 Chron. 33 11-20—Manasseh's Trial at Babylon before Asshurbanipal.

SENNACHERIB died in 681 B.C. (2 Kings 19 37); Hezekiah, it is supposed, fifteen years earlier, in 696; and Isaiah passed away, probably, about the latter date. With the disappearance of these chief actors, the curtain falls upon the great scenes of Judæan history which filled the last quarter of the eighth century. The only extant word of Isaiah that claims for its utterance a later epoch than 701 B.C., the year of Sennacherib's overthrow, is the oracle of ch. 19 23-25 (see pp. 88, 131), which reflects a state of things such as ensued upon Sennacherib's retreat from Palestine, when the hope of enduring peace might be entertained.

But the calm that followed upon the great deliverance of Jerusalem was of short duration. On Hezekiah's death the heathen party in Judah, kept under for a generation, seized the reins of power. Manasseh, a mere boy of twelve, grew up under its influence, and proved the complete opposite of his father in disposition and the worst enemy that the faith of his people had ever known. He renewed, in more thorough-going fashion, the attempts of his grandfather Ahaz to conform the national religion to that of the imperial power. Every kind of idolatrous practice he fostered, taking a pleasure in outraging the monotheistic sentiment, and turning the temple on Mount Zion into a veritable pantheon. The resistance of the conservatives and the denunciations of the prophets the king suppressed by violent persecutions, carried to the length, as it appears, of a wholesale massacre, in which the flower of the spiritual life of Israel was cut off: "Manasseh shed innocent blood very much, till he had filled Jerusalem from one end to another."

The account of Manasseh's reign given us in

2 Kings 21 1-18 presents a picture of unrelieved turpitude, and disaster for the true religion : "He did that which was evil in the sight of Jehovah, after the abominations of the heathen, whom Jehovah cast out before the children of Israel. For he built again the high places which Hezekiah his father had destroyed; and he reared up altars for Baal and made an Asherah, as did Ahab, king of Israel." Not content with reverting to the indigenous Canaanite paganism, Manasseh imported the adoration of the heavenly bodies, which formed the basis of Assyrian religion. "He worshipped all the host of heaven and served them. . . . He built altars for all the host of heaven in the two courts of Jehovah's house." The allusions of Zeph. 1 5, Jer. 7 18 44 17 ff., show that this fashionable cultus took root in Jerusalem and continued even after the Captivity. Thus Manasseh, it is said, "seduced" his people "to do that which is evil more than did the nations whom Jehovah destroyed before the children of Israel." There was, in fact, a general revolt against the austere simplicity and moral severity of Jehovistic faith; and the nation relapsed into the passionate sensualism of the Baalite worship, which always had a fascination for its lower classes, who were largely of Canaanite stock, while it welcomed no less the

more imposing and intellectual forms of Nature-worship, that came in with the Assyrian conquerors from the ancient shrines and seats of Eastern wisdom. The protracted reign of this monarch—lasting for fifty-five years, the longest in Israelite annals—secured full play for his policy and enabled him to inoculate the Judæans thoroughly with the heathen poison. The fact that Manasseh held the throne for so long and enforced the new régime so successfully, despite the powerful Isaianic traditions and the stout resistance which the orthodox party was bound to offer, argues him a man of ability and resolution; we know nothing from the Book of Kings of any foreign complications or military disasters suffered under his reign, such as the sacred author would surely have noted if calamities of this nature had befallen the apostate king. (To the story of Manasseh's captivity, found in Chronicles, we shall refer later.)

We take Manasseh to have been a skilful time-server, and what might be called a sensible man of the world. For him it was the cardinal point of policy to stand well with the Ninevite over-lord, who had quickly recovered, and even increased, his prestige in the west after the defeat of the year 701. A little principality like Judah could not afford to stand aloof, maintaining pretensions which were well enough in the days of David and Solomon, but were now antiquated and ridiculous. Manasseh aimed at bringing his people into line with surrounding nations; he sought to establish in the wrong way those prosperous relations between Judah and her neighbours which Isaiah had contemplated with delight, in what was probably his final vision (ch. 19 23-25; see p. 88), when he saw Israelites, Egyptians, and Assyrians worshipping together, and "Israel" as "a third with Egypt and with Assyria, a blessing in the midst of the earth." Unity was to be brought about not by spiritual conquest, but by concession and comprehension. *The religion of Jehovah*, Manasseh rightly perceived, was the force which kept the nation apart and had made foreign alliances impossible; this obstacle he was determined to break down. His plan succeeded only too well. The work of Isaiah and Hezekiah was for the time undone. The Southern Israelites became as steeped in idolatry, and as much demoralised by its vices, as the Northern Israelites a century earlier; so that Josiah's subsequent reformation could take no more than a temporary and superficial effect.

The doom of the Judæan nation, and of the house of David, was fixed from this date; and it is to *Manasseh* that later prophecy attributes

THE REACTION UNDER MANASSEH

the overthrow of Jerusalem which ensued half a century after his death. Accordingly, the historian of 2 Kings 23 26. 27, in completing his account of Josiah's reforms, continues, "Notwithstanding Jehovah turned not from the fierceness of His great wrath—because of all the provocations that Manasseh had provoked Him withal. And Jehovah said, I will remove Judah also out of My sight, as I have removed Israel; and I will cast off this city, even Jerusalem, and the house of which I have said, My name shall be there." Again, on the occasion of Nebuchadrezzar's first attack upon Jerusalem, his comment is: "This came on Judah . . . for the sin of Manasseh, according to all that he did, and also for the innocent blood that he shed." Jeremiah held the same view of Manasseh's culpability; Jehovah says through him, in pronouncing "this people" guilty of the unpardonable sin (Jer. 15 4): "I will cause them to be tossed to and fro among all the kingdoms of the earth, because of Manasseh, the son of Hezekiah, king of Judah, for that which he did in Jerusalem." Manasseh thus occupies in Judah the bad eminence of Jeroboam and Ahab in the history of the northern kingdom, as the seducer of his people from the true God and the author of the national ruin,

Manasseh's reign put an end to the futile conspiracies of the Judæan politicians, in league with Egypt, against the power of Assyria. In all other respects it proved a tragic reversal of Isaiah's policy, and dashed this great prophet's hope that a new, cleansed Jerusalem, a holy city of Jehovah, would issue from the fires of judgement through which his people passed during Sennacherib's invasion. It was a fond and too sanguine anticipation, when Micah and Isaiah imagined the Messianic age as lying immediately beyond the calamities of their own generation, and as ushered in forthwith by the " breaking " of the Assyrian " in Jehovah's land." How could they construe the future otherwise? They discerned the coming glory mounting above the limits of their stormy day; its *distance* they could not guess; and they searched in vain to know "what manner of time the Spirit which was in them did signify." The prophets were situated in regard to the first coming, as the apostles subsequently in regard to the second coming of the Lord: in each case the grand finalé bounded the outlook and loomed above the temporal horizon of the inspired men of the day; perspective was wanting, and for the intervening spaces they had no criterion of measurement. The nationalistic elements in the teaching of the prophets of the seventh century were the shell that had to be broken and cast away, so that the spiritual essence and seed of their ministry might live and expand, working on through future ages and sown upon a wider field.

Whether Isaiah survived to witness the reaction and to taste the bitterness of disappointment, we do not know. One prefers to think that "God kindly veiled his eyes." There is an apocryphal Jewish writing entitled *The Ascension of Isaiah*, preserved in Ethiopic, which professes to relate how the prophet was martyred by being "sawn asunder" in Manasseh's presence; the same tradition appears in the Talmud, and is perhaps alluded to in Hebrews 11 37; but its historical character is doubtful. When Jeremiah wrote (2 30), "Your own sword hath devoured your prophets," he was probably referring to the murders of Manasseh, resembling those perpetrated by Jezebel in Elijah's time; and Isaiah, if he lived so long as this, would be the first victim marked for destruction. The story referred to, whether founded on fact or otherwise, reflects truly the relations of the Hezekian and Manassite epochs and the ruthless spirit in which Manasseh dealt with everything that belonged to Isaiah's name and influence. To this unhappy cause the mutilated condition of the prophet's writings may plausibly be ascribed. Manasseh and his abettors would be well aware of the importance attaching to these documents (see Isa. 8 16. 17 30 8); they had every motive for destroying them. Isaiah's papers were preserved only in fugitive and imperfect copies, which the compilers of later times have had to piece together as well as they could.

The thoroughness and violence of the Manassite revolution are astonishing to us, and somewhat difficult to account for. Something was due, no doubt, to the lassitude consequent on a supreme effort. Patriotism and religious fervour had been excited to a feverish pitch; the spirit of the people was strained to the uttermost by the long struggle culminating with Sennacherib's disaster in the year 701. It proved with the Judæans as with England after Waterloo and the close of the Napoleonic wars. The intoxication of victory was followed by a period of moral and material exhaustion, which laid the people open to every temptation. It is sadly clear from Isaiah's reproofs uttered in the midst of the war (see ch. 22 12-14), that no regeneration was effected during its course, and that the purifying through judgement he had always looked for was not taking place. And when the tension was removed and the king and people surveyed the position in which they were left by Sennacherib's retreat, the gratefulness of relief gave place to a sense of disillusion, to chagrin and despondency, such as that which seized the Israelites in the desert after the exodus from Egypt. The glowing hopes raised by Isaiah were far indeed from being realized. The population had been decimated; the country was stripped bare up to the walls of the capital (see pp. 15–17 above). One Assyrian army had perished; but the Assyrian empire remained, and Sennacherib's arm was still strong in Palestine. Even after his deliverance, Hezekiah did not dare to renounce allegiance to Nineveh; and Manasseh gave pledges of complete subjection. Instead of the oppressor's yoke being broken from the neck of Israel, before many years it was more firmly fixed than ever. In 670 B.C. Esarhaddon accomplished the task of conquering Egypt, in which his father Sennacherib had been foiled, and the famous city of Thebes (the No-Amon of Nahum 3 s) fell before the Assyrian arms in 664. Through the first half of the seventh century Palestine remained quiescent under the Assyrian rule. Zidon, indeed, rebelled in 679, and Tyre, allied with Egypt, in 672; but both risings were unsuccessful. By the year 660 the dominion of Assyria attained its widest extent, stretching from the Persian Gulf to the Euxine, and from the Caspian Sea to Lydia in the west and Ethiopia in the south. This state of things, it might very plausibly be said, belied altogether Isaiah's predictions. Certainly "the Lord delayed His coming" as the destroyer of Assyria, and seemed to be "slack concerning His promise!" The gods of Asshur had proved themselves, after all, more than a match for Jehovah; and it was for prudent men to bow to circumstances and to confess the victory of "the host of heaven" over the local deities, granting them the place in the national temple which they had won by their worshippers' prowess. The time had come, Manasseh's advisers urged, frankly to acknowledge the religious along with the political ascendency of Assyria.

The new king appeared to stand therefore for breadth of mind and common sense, as against the exclusiveness and fierce intolerance of the Jehovist creed. He did not proscribe the cultus of Jehovah; but he required Him, like other deities, to acknowledge His fellows, and above all the imperial gods of the east. Dwellers in Jerusalem—natives and strangers—must be free to follow their convictions in matters of worship. The bigots and fanatics who obstructed progress and would defy the whole world for their one idea of the sole godhead of Jehovah, must be swept aside to make room for a larger statesmanship and a reconciliation with the ruling forces of the age. So we may interpret, in modern language, the reasons which lay behind the Assyrianising movement of Manasseh's reign; such were the principles of the dominant heathen party in Jerusalem, who had their successors in the Hellenistic faction against which the Maccabees rose in the second century before Christ. The tide ran strongly toward religious syncretism. Weary of the incessant perils and terrors of the last century, the people were ready to abandon the proud isolation which had cost them so dearly. Jerusalem craved for peace at any price; and Judah with her neighbours sank, under the weight of Assyrian domination, into a torpor which lasted for two generations.

Hence the history of David's kingdom, so vivid and stirring up to this point, becomes a blank from the overthrow of Sennacherib to the accession of Josiah. It was a period of spiritual arrest and of moral winter. The voice of inspiration was silenced: "the sword" of Manasseh, powerless against foreign enemies, had "devoured the prophets like a destroying lion." The only prophecy that can with any certainty be assigned to Judæa in Manasseh's time is found in the two pathetic closing chapters of the Book of Micah, which were either written by that prophet in his retired old age, or by some successor belonging to the same region of the Shephelah and breathing Micah's spirit (see Vol. I, pp. 263-270). The question, "Shall I give my firstborn for my transgression, the fruit of my body for the sin of my soul?" belonged to the time when the human sacrifices offered to Molech were in vogue; and Manasseh himself, according to 2 Chron. 33 6, had recourse to this frightful practice, "making his children to pass through the fire in the valley of the son of Hinnom,"—the ravine below Jerusalem from which the name *Ge-henna* (valley of Hinnom) was derived. Social dissolution has never been described in more graphic and melancholy language than that of Mic. 7 1-6 :

Woe, woe is me!
For I am become like sweepings of harvest, like gleanings of the vintage—
Not a cluster to eat, not a fig that my soul lusteth after!
Perished are the leal from the land; of the upright among men there is none!
All of them are lurking for blood; every man takes his brother in a net.
Their hands are on evil, to do it thoroughly.

> The prince maketh requisition; the judge judgeth for payment; and the great man, he speaketh his lust:
> So together they weave it out.
> The best of them is but a thorn thicket; the most upright worse than a prickly hedge.
>
> * * * * *
>
> Trust not any friend! rely on no confidant! from her that lies in thy bosom guard the gates of thy mouth!
> For son insulteth father; daughter is risen against her mother; daughter-in-law against her mother-in-law;
> And the enemies of a man are the men of his house.
> (G. A. Smith's *Book of the Twelve Prophets*.)

The plaintive prophet, like Elijah in Ahab's time, seems to himself to stand alone in the moral waste, the solitary monument of a better day. Yet out of the depth of winter he predicts the coming spring (vv. 7. 8):

> But as for me, for Jehovah will I spy out! I will wait for the God of my salvation:
>   My God shall hear me!
> Rejoice not over me, O mine enemy:
>   Though I be fallen, I rise again!
>   Though I sit in darkness, Jehovah is a light unto me!

This unquenchable light of Jehovah, shining in Israel's gloomiest hour, may be seen in Psalms that bear the stamp of the same evil time, when the godly were objects of contempt and persecution to their fellow countrymen and society was filled with treachery and mistrust: see Pss. 36, 55, 64, 140-142, assigned by Ewald and others to the period of the dissolution of the Judæan monarchy. If, as many of the soundest critics suppose,[1] the Book of Deuteronomy in its existing form was the product of the time of Manasseh, this fact would afford the strongest evidence of the powers of recuperation slumbering in the soul of Israel through this period of seeming death. The leading ideas and motives developed in Deuteronomy are such as run directly counter to the forces active in the Manassite reaction. Its "tender, thoughtful, evangelical spirit" is the very spirit which inspires Micah 6 and 7, the characteristic oracle of this period. Through tribulation and defeat the prophetic temper has become, since Isaiah's day, more gentle, more subdued, more inward and reflective, more patiently hopeful.

There can be little doubt that the volume of Deuteronomy (chs. 5-26)—prepared, as may be supposed, in secret and hidden in the temple during Manasseh's tyranny—was the book of the law discovered by Hilkiah as it is related

---

[1] See Smith's *Dict. of the Bible* (2nd ed.), or Hastings' *D.B.*, on Deuteronomy; also Harper's "Deuteronomy" in *The Expositor's Bible*, ch. ii, "The Historical Setting of Deuteronomy."

in 2 Kings 22 8. 10-13, 23 21, which supplied the basis of Josiah's reformation and a starting-point for subsequent religious developments. Deuteronomy was, in fact, the beginning of the Jewish Scripture, the first book of the Old Testament to be canonized (though by no means the first to be composed) and accepted as the popular written standard of national faith and duty. Granting this construction of the inner history of Israel to be correct, the age of Manasseh, which appears so barren, was in reality amongst the most productive in the course of revelation.

The prophet Nahum, who will be the subject of our next chapter, lived toward the close of this period; but his eyes were turned wholly in the direction of Nineveh. He has nothing to say about home affairs and the religious condition of his own people. The one message he sends to Jerusalem, as if from a distance, is that of congratulation on the expected overthrow of "the bloody city," from whose rapacity and cruelty she has suffered for so long. Announcing this event he cries, "Behold upon the mountains the feet of him that bringeth good tidings, that publisheth peace!" (1 15); it is in this form and connexion that the word "gospel" (good tidings) first appears in Scripture. Nahum's outburst is proof, at any rate, of the awaking in Israel of the old prophetic rage against Assyria.

The Second Book of Chronicles (33 11-20) adds a supplementary chapter to the life of Manasseh, which is of singular interest. It relates how he was seized and brought in chains to meet the Assyrian king in Babylon, where "in" his "distress he sought Jehovah his God and humbled himself greatly before the God of his fathers."[1] Upon this repentance, we are told, Manasseh was restored to his throne, whereupon he removed the idolatrous symbols from Jerusalem and "com-

---

[1] The Chronicler refers in vv. 18, 19 to the "prayer of Manasseh," made in his prison at Babylon, in terms implying that it was extant in his time, being "written among the acts of the kings of Israel" and "in the history of Hozai" (or "the seers"); but he does not cite its words. The defect some Hellenistic Jew, living probably not long before the Christian era, attempted to supply by composing the "Prayer of Manasses," which was handed down by some copies of the Greek and Latin Bibles, and is also contained in the *Apostolic Constitutions*. This composition is "a fine penitential prayer," in style and spirit not unworthy of the place given to it in the Bible of the Early Church; but it is purely Apocryphal, and a work of imagination. In the Greek (LXX) Bible MSS. containing it, the Prayer stands amongst the Canticles appended to the Psalter; the Latin copies attach it to 2 Chronicles. The Greek text does not appear to be based on any Hebrew original; nor can its existence be traced in Rabbinical tradition. See the articles on the subject in Smith's or Hastings' *Dictionary of the Bible*.

manded Judah to serve Jehovah the God of Israel." At the same time, Jerusalem was re-fortified and the military strength of the country increased. And so Manasseh made, after all, an edifying end!

The historicity of this narrative is much disputed.[1] No hint of the conversion is given in the Book of Kings, where Josiah is represented as purging the temple and abolishing the foreign worships, as though these had remained in full activity up to his accession; and Jeremiah refers to Manasseh with unqualified condemnation. The story of Chronicles, however, is fairly reconciled with other accounts (1) by supposing that Manasseh's repentance came too late to amend the mischief of his life and to stay the apostasy, and for this reason is ignored in the Book of Kings; and (2) by observing that Manasseh's son Amon (Josiah's father), during his brief reign of two years, "walked in all the ways that his father had walked in, and served the idols that his father served. He forsook Jehovah, the God of his fathers, and walked not in the ways of Jehovah" (2 Kings 21 19-22); "he humbled not himself before Jehovah, as Manasseh his father

[1] See e.g. Prof. A. S. Peake in Hastings' *D.B.*, article "Manasseh."

had humbled himself" (2 Chron. 33 23). There took place, it appears, a counter-reformation under Amon; and whatever effect the father's belated return to the national faith had produced, was neutralized by the son's infidelity. So the reformers who surrounded Josiah found idolatry as rampant as it had been in the worst days of his grandfather.

There is no great improbability in Manasseh's having received such treatment from his suzerain as the Chronicler describes, notwithstanding his long-maintained vassalage. This Judæan king is named in a list of Esarhaddon's (who reigned from 681 to 668), and again of Asshurbanipal's (668–626), as amongst the tribute-payers of the empire in the west—he stands in each instance second in the enumeration, between the king of Tyre and the king of Edom. During the latter part of Asshurbanipal's protracted reign civil war broke out in 648–7 B.C., when Manasseh had ruled nearly fifty years, between himself and his brother Sammaghes (or Shamashumakin, p. 179), viceroy of Babylon.[1] It is stated in Asshurbanipal's record of this struggle that, amongst others, "the kings of the west country [which means

---

[1] Babylon was cruelly destroyed by Sennacherib in the year 689, on its second capture by him. But the great city had been restored and treated with favour by Esarhaddon.

Phœnicia and Palestine] he [Sammaghes] seduced to revolt from me; with him they made common cause." Egypt, as we should expect, was involved in this wide-spread combination. The rebellion was repressed, and if, as we may presume, Manasseh was a party to it, his disgrace and trial before the over-lord in Babylon were the inevitable sequel. There had been, however, no revolt on his part from Assyria; his misfortune was to choose amiss between two Assyrian rulers. Manasseh's name does not figure in the inscription of Asshurbanipal relating to the affair; but the treatment he received, as it is described in Chronicles—in being first brought in chains before the great king, and then released and restored to power—has a parallel in the case of the contemporary Pharaoh-Necho of Egypt, who (according to the inscriptions) had this very experience under the same circumstances.[1] Punishment and threatened deposition at the hands of the Assyrians, to whom he had been subservient all his life and for whose favour he had sacrificed his fathers' faith and his country's honour, were a humiliation calculated, above everything, to convince the old king of the folly of his ways and to cure him of his infatuation for foreign gods.

[1] See Schrader's *Cuneiform Inscriptions*, vol. ii, pp. 53-59.

CHAPTER XIX

NAHUM, AND THE FALL OF NINEVEH

The Assyrian Empire after 701 B.C. — Esarhaddon's Character—Conquest of Egypt—Culmination and Decline of Assyrian Power—Rise of the Medes—Scythian Migration—Assyrian Kings after Asshurbanipal—Causes of Nineveh's Overthrow—Purport of Nahum's Prophecy—Nahum's Birthplace—Date of Nahum—Criticism of the Book—Supposed Alphabetic Poem—Antique Style of chap. 1—Connexion of ch. 1 with chs. 2 and 3—Literary Quality of the Book—Nahum 1 1-10 a Psalm—Order of 1 11-2 2—Analysis of chs. 2, 3—Features of Nahum's Warsong—Nineveh's Cruelty and Cunning—Geographical and Historical Notes—The Author an Eye-witness—Analysis.

FOR a whole century after Isaiah's prediction the downfall of the Assyrian empire lingered and its "damnation slumbered." Sennacherib's disaster on the borders of Egypt and the foiling of his attempt on Jerusalem (see pp. 15-16, 120-1) proved but a temporary check to the advance of Assyrian arms. Judæa, indeed, kept its national existence, and Jerusalem, perhaps through some religious fear, remained unviolated by military occupation. But the Judæan king returned to his allegiance as a feudatory of Nineveh; Manasseh for most of his reign showed himself an obsequious vassal. So far as we can gather, Sennacherib was occupied for the twenty years through which he survived the defeat of 701 with expeditions in other parts of the empire,[1] and meddled no further with Egypt, which remained under the dominion of the powerful Ethiopian ruler Tirhakah (Isa. 18 1. 2 20 3-5 37 9). Palestine was mainly important to the Assyrians as a stepping-stone to Egypt, and so long as its princes paid tribute and refrained from intrigues against the suzerain, they were little disturbed. Sennacherib in his later years was engaged in long and exhausting struggles with the Chaldæans, headed by the able and indefatigable Merodach-baladan (see Isa. 39), and with the Elamites. He ended his military career by the complete destruction of Babylon—captured, for

[1] Some recent scholars hold, however, that the double account appearing in Isa. 36 1-37 8 and 37 9-37 relates to *two* abortive assaults on Jerusalem, taking place in 701 and 690-1 respectively. One must admit that Isa. 37 38 looks in favour of this view; its connexion with ver. 37 suggests that Sennacherib's murder was the immediate sequel of his retreat from the borders of Egypt. But see p. 16 above.

the second time during his reign (see pp. 89, 168), in the year 689. The city was rebuilt ten years later by his son Esarhaddon (who had a Babylonian mother), and quickly regained its prosperity.

The great Sennacherib fell by the murderous hands of two of his sons (see Isa. 37 38; 2 Kings 19 37). The third son, Esarhaddon, emerged victorious from the civil war that ensued. He proved the best of the Sargonid line. Apart from the passage just referred to recording his accession, there is but a single allusion to Esarhaddon (681–668 B.C.) in the Old Testament: the foreign Samaritans more than a century and a half later remembered him, according to their words quoted in Ezra 4 2, as "the king of Assyria who had brought them" into Palestine—he appears to have settled a *second* colony of Eastern captives (following the first of 721 B.C.) in the territory of Northern Israel.[1] With this later plantation we should probably connect the interesting account in 2 Kings 17 24-34 of the restoration of Jehovah's worship in Samaria; the despatch of an exiled priest of Jehovah to teach the immigrants "the

---

[1] Ver. 10 appears to indicate a *third* plantation, under the next Assyrian king, Asshurbanipal, who is almost certainly meant by "the great and noble Osnapper."

manner of the God of the land" accords with what is known of the conciliatory character of Esarhaddon. This intervention in Palestine may be connected with Esarhaddon's war against Egypt in 674–670 B.C.

After he had rebuilt Babylon and composed the affairs of the empire in the east, Esarhaddon returned to the task of subduing Egypt, which his father Sennacherib had been compelled to abandon. The increasing discontent of the Egyptians under the Ethiopian yoke, and the decline of Tirhakah's vigour, facilitated the enterprise, which this time proved successful. The first attack, made in 674, miscarried, and its failure led to the rebellion of Tyre and of several Aramæan states. Disturbances on his northern frontier compelled further delay on Esarhaddon's part. But in 670 he marched with an overwhelming force across the desert, defeated Tirhakah on his own ground, and took Memphis (*Noph* in Isa. 19 13, etc.; *Moph* in Hos. 9 6), the metropolis of Lower Egypt, by assault. The whole of the Delta thus fell under Assyrian domination. Tirhakah, however, recovered Memphis in the following year, and Esarhaddon was on his way to avenge this loss when he died in the year 668. His army, notwithstanding, continued its march, recaptured Memphis and thoroughly subdued the lower Nile valley, Tirhakah fleeing far up the river to his native capital of Napata; the campaign ended with the submission of Thebes, the world-famous mistress of Upper Egypt. Tirhakah died soon after this; but his successor recovered the Thebaid and drove out the Assyrians once more from the Nile valley, reoccupying Memphis.

The triumph of the new Ethiopian king was of short duration, and proved the last won by his dynasty in Egypt. In 664 Asshurbanipal invaded the country in person, and carried everything before him until he came to Thebes, which his troops sacked and destroyed in the most savage way. This magnificent city, whose fame reaches back to the dawn of history and finds a place in the *Iliad*—Homer's "hundred-gated Thebes"—received a fatal blow, which resounds in the lines of Nahum (3 8-10), her fate serving as a prophecy for that of her pitiless destroyer:

Art thou [Nineveh] to fare better than No-Amon,—
She that dwelt amid the Nile-channels with the waters encircling her,
Whose rampart was the sea—the waters her wall?
Cush[1] was her strength, and Mizraim without end;
Phut[2] and the Lybians came to her help.

[1] *I.e.* Ethiopia, the region south of Egypt—modern Nubia and Soudan.

[2] Probably the Somali coast.

Even she was doomed to exile; she hath gone into captivity.
Yea, her little ones were dashed to pieces at every street corner;
And over her nobles they cast lots, and her great men were chained with fetters.

Isaiah's predictions of the conquest of Egypt by Asshur were at last amply fulfilled (chs. 18, 20). For some years Egypt remained the passive subject of Assyria. The year 660 saw the empire of Nineveh at the climax of its dominion; it stretched unbroken from the Euxine and Caspian to the cataracts of the Nile, and from the river Halys to the Persian Gulf. Five hundred years or more it had taken the Assyrian power to climb to this summit; in fifty years it fell! The reign of Asshurbanipal (the Greek Sardanapalus: 668–626 B.C.) opened with the conquest of Thebes, the proudest achievement of Assyrian arms; it closed witnessing Nineveh herself driven to bay and fighting for bare life. Two chief causes brought about this swift reversal of fortune. A new imperial power had risen in the east. The Median tribes, whose home was the table-land of Iran south of the Caspian and who formed along with the Persians the Iranian branch of the Aryan family of peoples, had been welded by the early part of the seventh century into a single nation, ruled by an able dynasty which established its capital at Ecbatana. This young and vigorous people learnt the lessons of military organization by conflict with the Assyrians, and by the middle of the century was able to hold its own against them.

Somewhat earlier than this there took place one of those obscure movements in the heart of Asia, which have again and again driven its hordes from their barren steppes over the civilized lands of the south and west. These invaders, who poured into Europe over the Danube and into South-Western Asia by the passes of the Caucasus, or rounded the Caspian Sea from the east, were known to the Greeks in some of their bodies as "Cimmerians," but more generally, and somewhat vaguely, as "Scythians."[1] They are the "Gog and Magog" of Ezekiel: the deep impression they left on after-times is shown by his oracles against them in chs. 38 and 39, which are echoed in the Revelation of John (20 7-9). To their coming the gloomy prophecy of

[1] It seems likely that the "Cimmerians" of Grecian history (not improbably identified with the "Cimbri" whom the Romans encountered about 100 B.C., and again with the Celtic "Cymry") were an Aryan people distinct from the Scythians, who had been propelled into Central and Western Europe by the Scythians (? Tartars) driving them from their earlier seats north of the Euxine.

Zephaniah relates (see Vol. III, Chap. XXI). For above twenty years the Scythians held the west of Asia in terror, overrunning with their swarms of light horsemen all the lowlands between the Armenian mountains and the borders of Egypt, where at last their progress stayed. This Scythian deluge accelerated the political changes coming over Western Asia. The nomad invaders made few settlements anywhere; they recoiled from fortified cities, and made little impression on mountainous districts like Judæa; but the rich plains of Mesopotamia and Syria were thoroughly ravaged, and the whole commerce of these regions for the time was ruined.

In 635 the Median king Phraortes renounced the Assyrian lordship and declared war against Asshurbanipal. The resistance proved surprisingly feeble; in a few campaigns the entire mountain-region east of the Tigris was wrested from Ninevite rule. The old Assyrian lion seemed all at once to have lost his fighting powers. From the vantage-ground thus gained, the Medes were in a position to strike at the heart of their mighty foe. Asshurbanipal's troops were driven in upon the angle between the Zab and the Tigris rivers, which formed a natural fortress, the ancient rallying-ground of the forces of Asshur. Despite a severe defeat, in which

Phraortes fell, the Medes appear to have pressed on their attack under his son Cyaxares; they blockaded Nineveh and its capture seemed within sight (625), when they were called home by the irruption of the Scythians from the north into their own country. This sudden intervention, due probably to an alliance made with the barbarians by the Assyrian Government, saved Nineveh for the time, but at the expense of a heavier ruin for her in the end.[1]

The Assyrian records become broken and uncertain after 626, the year of Asshurbanipal's death. For long it was supposed, on the strength of Herodotus' account, in Book I, §§ 102 f., of his *Histories*, that the Medes overthrew Nineveh at this crisis (*c.* 625 B.C.); but it now appears

---

[1] We have followed the account of the decline and fall of Nineveh given in Maspero's *Histoire Ancienne des Peuples de l'Orient*, in accordance with most modern authorities. It should be stated, however, that the two latest German commentators on *Nahum*, Nowack and Marti, reject the hypothesis of a *double* siege of Nineveh, founded on the combination of Herodotus' story with the data of the monuments. They suppose the first attack of the Medes, before 625, to have terminated with the defeat and death of Phraortes. On this view, Nahum prophesied when the final assault of Cyaxares was approaching, about 610. Some reasons for maintaining the earlier date are given below. A. R. S. Kennedy (art. "Nahum" in Hastings' *D.B.*) puts the occasion of the Book as far back as 645 B.C.

that Asshur enjoyed a respite, while the Medes were held in check by the Scythians. Two shadowy names close the long succession of Assyrian monarchs — that of Asshuredililani (626-620), and of Sinshariskun (Greek *Saracus*, 620-606) who burnt himself alive in his palace to escape the hands of the Medes. The Scythians once expelled, Cyaxares the Mede resumed the attack upon Nineveh, with Nabopalassar, the revolted viceroy of Babylon, for his ally; and the old warrior city, deserted and impoverished, fell an easy victim to this second onslaught. Since that date Nineveh and her sister cities have lain in utter ruin, their very site unknown until the explorer's spade discovered them half a century ago.

The swift descent of Assyria under Asshurbanipal was due partly to the enervating effect of vast wealth immorally acquired, but chiefly to the exhaustion of her fighting caste by the incessant wars which her bad government entailed (see Vol. I, pp. 242-244), and her consequent dependence upon mercenary forces. After the conquest of Egypt in 664, the old feuds with Elam and Babylon broke out again. Esarhaddon had left the possession of the refounded Babylon to a younger son, Shamashumakin, under Asshurbanipal's supremacy. About the year 650 the

Babylonian brother rebelled, and Asshurbanipal found himself confronted with a wide-spread conspiracy. Babylon was captured, and severely punished, in 648; the Elamite country was ravaged and its ancient monarchy destroyed in 646—leaving the field free in that direction, as it proved, for the expansion of Media. Thus Asshur once more emerged victorious from a desperate struggle with her hereditary foes, and registered great victories on her memorial slabs; but it was for the last time. She was only less spent than her prostrate enemies; she abandoned Egypt, which had seized the opportunity to rebel under Psammetichus. In Asia Minor, too, the Assyrian troops retreated; the boundaries of the empire were shrinking on all sides, before the Median war broke out in 635. Asshur was already a spent force.

The Book of Nahum signalizes this historical epoch. It is *the oracle of Jehovah's triumph over Nineveh*, and stands in the same relation to the fate of the Assyrian power as Exod. 15 to the overthrow of Pharaoh, and as Isa. 13, 14, with Jer. 50–51 and Ps. 137, to the fall of Babylon. The little volume, of forty-seven verses, bears on this one theme with concentrated passion. The line of prediction which ran through Isa. 10 $_{5-34}$ 14 $_{24-27}$ 30 $_{27-33}$ 36, 37, and was interrupted by Manasseh's philo-Assyrian reign, culminates here. Nahum has no word to say of Israel's future, of her sins or punishment, nor of the Messianic hope—he is unquoted in the New Testament. We have no better means of knowing his thoughts upon these matters than we should have had in Isaiah's case, had the passages above mentioned alone survived out of his writings. With this limited material before us, we ought not to infer Nahum's indifference, much less his opposition, to the contemporary doctrines of Zephaniah and Jeremiah. He strikes but one chord in the harmony of prophetic song, but he strikes it with splendid decision and energy. The only allusions made to the poet's own people are in chap. 1 13. 15 (Heb. 2 1) and 2 2 (Heb. ver. 3):

Now will I break his yoke from upon thee, and his bonds
    will I snap in sunder.
Behold, upon the mountains the feet of the bringer of
    good news!
  Keep thy feasts, O Judah, fulfil thy vows;
For never again shall the wicked one pass through thee—
    he is utterly cut off!
For Jehovah restoreth the excellency of Jacob, as the
    excellency of Israel;[1]

[1] *Jacob* appears to stand here for *Judah*, as in Isa. 46 3 and Ob. 18; so that Nahum looks for a complete restoration, of South and North, on the overthrow of the Ninevite dominion.

When plunderers had left them empty, and destroyed their vine-branches.[1]

Nahum has no message but of *consolation* for Israel; it is curious that his name bears just this meaning in Hebrew—the " consoler."

Nahum is entitled "the Elkoshite" (Heb. *'Elqoshi*), as his predecessor in the Canon is "Micah the Morashtite" (see Vol. I, p. 246). Unfortunately in this case the local designation does not help us much. There is (1) a modern *Elkúsh* (or *Elkósh*), some distance north of Mosul, which lies near the site of Nineveh, where stands a tomb of the prophet frequented by Jews, Muhammadans, and Christians. But its tradition dates only from the sixteenth century; and the name of the village, which probably gave birth to the tradition, is said to be of Arabic extraction. This spot is, however, favoured by scholars who, like Ewald, find Assyrian words in Nahum's dialect and recognize in his descriptions the marks of local colour and of acquaintance with the military situation. Against this conjecture it is argued that the author shows himself a Judæan, and

[1] These verses should be read continuously (so Marti, G. A. Smith, and other commentators). By some accident they have been interspersed with verses addressed to Assyria (see p. 192 below).

makes no allusion to the kingdom of the Ten Tribes (see, however, ch. 2 2, with the note upon it above), whereas the exiles settled in Assyria were Northern Israelites. The knowledge that the prophet shows of Nineveh and of Assyrian warfare, like that he shows of No-Amon (3 8f.), hardly goes beyond what was common property in the empire; Judæans, moreover, during the peaceful times of Manasseh's reign, may well have visited the great city. The two or three supposed Assyrian words in his Book are of doubtful reading. (2) Jerome discovered Nahum's Elkosh in "a hamlet in Galilee," pointed out to him by a Jewish guide, bearing the name *Helkesei*, which may perhaps be identical with the modern village of *El Kauze*, situated in the territory of Naphtali. If born in Northern Israel, amongst the remnant surviving the Assyrian deportation, Nahum might have emigrated to the south and identified himself with Judah. But there is no further confirmation of Jerome's view. (3) The New Testament *Capernaum* (Καφαρναούμ: Hebrew *Kaphar-Nachum*) has taken its name from this prophet or from some namesake, for the word signifies "Village of Nahum": no other Nahum is known in the Old Testament. (4) A fourth tradition, probably of early Syrian origin, is found in the *Vitæ Prophetarum* ascribed to Epiphanius, which associates this prophet with an *Elkesei* "of the tribe of Simeon," toward the south-east of Judæa. If he belonged to this neighbourhood, Nahum's home was not far from that of Micah the Morashtite (see Vol. I, pp. 246, 257); and it may be noted that the two prophets amongst "the Twelve" whose names bear local qualifications are neighbours in the Hebrew order of the Books. Whether a Judæan or not by birth, Nahum was such in sentiment: he associates himself passionately with the wrongs that Jehovah's people had suffered from the Assyrian. His poem is steeped in the spirit of religious patriotism; it is, like Exodus 15 or Psalm 68, a great national war-song.

The date of "the vision of Nahum" is determined on the one side by its reference to the fall of Thebes (3 8-10) in 664 B.C., and on the other by the fall of Nineveh herself, which happened in the year 607 or thereabouts. As we have intimated, Nineveh appears to have been twice invested by the Medes at an interval of twenty years—her capture in the first instance having been averted by the Scythian irruption. The scope of the prophecy points to the earlier crisis, rather than the later, as in prospect. Nineveh is still rich and powerful. No allusion is made to the Scythians (the enemy Nahum describes is of the regular military order and equipment), nor to the previous danger of the city—such reference we should have expected at any date subsequent to 625. Moreover, when the prophet writes, Judah is still under the "yoke" of Asshur and held in its "bonds," which was hardly the case, even in the most nominal sense, later than the above epoch; see 2 Kings 23 15-20, where King Josiah is seen exercising a free hand in Samarian territory. Long before her fall Nineveh had lost command of Palestine; as the Book of Zephaniah will show, after Manasseh's death it was the Scythian hordes, not now the troops of Assyria, that the Judæans had to fear. Nahum's favourable tone towards Judah is intelligible in the early reign of Josiah (who acceded in 640); at the same time, he shows no trace of the Deuteronomic style, which so much affected prophecy after 621 B.C. The nearer we can bring Nahum's date to 664, the better we understand his lively recollection of the fall of Egyptian Thebes. The turning-point of Assyria's fortunes came, as we have seen, about the year 640; with the outbreak of the Median war in 635, ruin was looming on the horizon and "the hammer" destined to shatter Nineveh had "come up before her face" (2 1). This seems to us the likeliest juncture for Nahum's pronouncement of doom—somewhere between the years 640 and 630, early in Josiah's reign, when the Medes were launching their first powerful blows at Assyria and before the arrival of the Scythians on the scene.

The Book is peculiar in having a double title: (a) *The Oracle* (or *Burden*) *of Nineveh*; (b) *The Book of the Vision of Nahum the Elkoshite*. The original heading, resembling the titles of the Book of Obadiah and of the First Book of Isaiah (see pp. 28–29), was simply, it is supposed, *The Vision of Nahum the Elkoshite*. The heading (*a*) prefixed to this is a subject-title, betraying the editor's hand, which brings the prophecy into line with Isa. 13–23 and with Habakkuk, the next in order; this addition necessitated the insertion of "The Book of" (before "the Vision," etc.)—which occurs in no other title amongst the Nebi'im. The twofold title is connected by some critics with the twofold strain that they find in the work. Until the last twelve years "Nahum" had escaped the dissecting knife. The text of chap. 1 was felt to be obscure in places; and the last five verses, along with the first two of ch. 2, seemed to have suffered disarrangement. But critics so decided as Ewald, Kuenen, Robertson Smith, Wellhausen, Driver, Cornill, suspected no diversity of authorship; they treated the three chapters as homogeneous.

In 1880 however, and more successfully in 1894, the German Dr Bickell, a high authority on Hebrew metres, pointed out traces of an alphabetic psalm in vv. 1-7, and attempted on the strength of this sequence to reconstruct a complete acrostic poem extending to ch. 2 2 (omitting ver. 1), which he supposed that some later editor has prefixed, in a mutilated form, to Nahum's original triumph-song. Bickell's discovery is endorsed, and variously worked out, by several leading Hebraists—by Hermann Gunkel in a very ingenious and thorough way;[1] others regard it with scepticism. The late A. B. Davidson pronounced that "such a theory can never be more than an academic exercise."[2] Dr Driver thinks that "the author allowed himself here and there, and perhaps half accidentally, to follow the alphabetical order." This is as much as can be made out from the succession of the letters as they stand, and without rewriting the chapter (as Drs Bickell and Gunkel actually do) to suit the hypothesis. On the assumption of the alphabetic scheme—such as appears, *e.g.*, in Psalms 9 and 10, 34, etc.—the composition is

---

[1] See "Nahum" in Hastings' *Dict. of the Bible*; also pp. 81-89 of G. A. Smith's *Book of the Twelve Prophets*, vol. ii.
[2] Introduction to Nahum, in his admirable work on *Nahum, Habakkuk, and Zephaniah*, in the *Cambridge Bible for Schools*,

referred to post-exilic times. (Upon this view, chapter 1 could, of course, supply no data for Nahum's situation; its references to the period would have been made from a distance.)

But the alphabetic style, admitting its presence here, is after all no certain mark by itself of late writing.[1] The tone and atmosphere of chap. 1 are those pervading the sequel; there is the same dignity and breadth of treatment, the same severity and fervour, the same terse energy and vivid colouring throughout the Book. The catchwords of the post-exilic Psalms are wanting, while striking parallels of language are found connecting the disputed passages with earlier Hebrew writing, especially with Isaiah.[2]

Nahum's pæan over ruined Nineveh could hardly be called "prophecy" nor have found a place in the roll of the Nebi'im, without the basis furnished by the exordium; for it would lack its theocratic ground and justification, and

[1] See Delitzsch's *Commentary on the Psalms*, Introduction to Ps. 9. The acrostic Pss. 9 and 10 (a single piece in the LXX) refer to Zion in a manner that seems to demand a date before the Judæan Exile.

[2] Comp. vv. 2. 3 with Ex. 20 5 34 6 and Ps. 18 9-13; ver. 4 with Isa. 33 9; ver. 5 with Hab. 3 6 and Jer. 4 24 (of Nahum's period —perhaps echoing him); ver. 7 with Ps. 46 1; ver. 8 with Isa. 30 28 8 22; ver. 12 with Isa. 10 33. 34; ver. 13 with Isa. 9 4 10 27 14 25. Isa. 52 7. 8 (exilic) we may take to be an expansion of Na. 1 15.

would stand in no definite connexion with the administration of God's kingdom in Israel; its religious lesson and moral would remain unenforced. Chap. 1 2-10, in fact, sets up the throne of the awful Judge of nations; vv. 11-15 declare the sentence He pronounces on the great criminal at His bar; then chs. 2 and 3 describe the execution of the sentence, which already begins to take effect—3 19 reiterating his crime at the conclusion. From its subject-matter "the oracle of Nineveh" may therefore be designated *the oracle of Jehovah's revenge upon Nineveh*: "Woe to the city of blood!" (3 1) is its key-note; and its finalé is the exclamation, "All that hear the report of thee, clap their hands over thee; for over whom hath not thy evil-doing passed continually?" (comp. Job 27 23). Thus Assyria is dismissed from the theatre of history, amid the execration of mankind voiced by Jehovah's prophet Nahum.

This little book ranks amongst the finest things in Hebrew literature. In poetic fire and sublimity it approaches the best work of Isaiah; Pusey speaks of "the grandeur, energy, power, and vividness of Nahum"—which however, as he says, are not "fully felt" except by the reader of the Hebrew. The frequent obscurity—*e.g.* in 1 10. 12 2 7. 8 3 7—due probably to errors of copying, mars the effect of Nahum's verses; but the unity of conception, the artistic handling of the theme, the wealth of metaphor and brilliance of description, the firm, swift movement, the vehemence of passion held in strict control which animates the poem, make themselves felt through the faulty text and the veil of translation. Amongst his characteristic lines are those of 1 3, "In storm and whirlwind is Jehovah's way, and the clouds are the dust of His feet"; 2 4, "the aspect of the [enemies'] chariots is like torches, like lightnings they dart to and fro." In 2 11-13, the Assyrian monarch in the days of his power is likened to "the lion" who "did tear in pieces for his whelps and strangled for his lionesses," who "filled his caves with prey and his dens with ravin"; the great city (3 4) was "the well-favoured harlot, mistress of sorceries"—this figure John's Apocalypse borrows for the benefit of Rome; its frontier fortresses prove as "fig-trees with figs early ripe," that "if shaken fall into the mouth of the eater" (3 12); its mercenary population are as "grasshoppers that camp in the hedges in the cold of the day," but "flee away as the sun grows hot, and none knows the place where they be" (3 17). Nahum first bids us "Behold on the mountains the feet of the bringer of good tidings, the publisher of peace" (1 15; Heb. 2 1)—the messenger who comes to Judah over the eastern hills with the longed-for news of Nineveh's capture: this watchword the later Isaiah took from his lips (Isa. 40 9 57 2), translating it into a nobler sense for Gospel use. We dwell upon these striking traits of Nahum, because he is neglected by the Bible-reader, and is never distinctly quoted in the New Testament. His prophecy was so single-minded, centring itself so completely upon its one subject, and it was so perfectly fulfilled in the immediate sequel, that it requires some historical reflexion to realize its place in Divine revelation and to understand the vital part which the judgement upon Nineveh played in the progress of the kingdom of God; comp. Isa. 25 1. 2, etc.

We have already touched on the difficulties attaching to ch. 1, and its connexion with chs. 2 and 3. Vv. 2-10 form a psalm rather than a prophecy, and supply the prelude of the Book. This song is of the type of Exod. 15, 1 Sam. 2 1-10, Pss. 46 and 48, 93, 97, celebrating the greatness of Jehovah as Lord of nature and Judge of the peoples. It is the "jealous and avenging God" of the Ten Words of Moses whom this crisis in human history reveals (ver. 2), whose "anger" is "slow," but whose power is always equal to the demands of His justice, as the forces of nature witness (vv. 3-6). His pity for Israel calls for this avenging; for "Jehovah is good, a stronghold in the day of trouble; and He knoweth them that put their trust in Him" (7)—the one touch of tenderness in this stern Book. Vv. 8-10 set forth under various figures, not altogether clear in the text as it stands, the finality of doom that must overtake the obstinately wicked.

Ver. 11, though obscure, seems to be a transition from the general doctrine of the foregoing psalm to the actual situation. It is addressed surely to *Nineveh*, and is therefore best read, according to the arrangement of the verses suggested by Davidson and Marti, along with vv. 12. 14 as supplying the immediate preface to chap. 2. Then vv. 13 and 15, with the addition of 2 2—all accosting *Judah*—make a clear sense running on from ver. 10: "*now* will I break his yoke," etc. (ver. 13), recalls the old pending prediction of Isa. 9 4 10 27. The readjusted paragraph fits in naturally between the prophet's song of praise to Jehovah and his prophecy of woe against Nineveh. What has led to the mixing up of Nahum's words of comfort to his people with his words of threatening to their enemies, it is impossible to say: that some such confusion has taken place seems obvious.

Chap. 2 (with the subtraction of ver. 2, and the

prefixing of ch. 1 11. 12. 14, which supply the theme of all that follows) and ch. 3 constitute the body of Nahum's work. Ch. 2 is *description*, depicting the investment (vv. 1. 3-5), assault and sack of the city (6-9), and the frightful desolation in which she is left (10-13); ch. 3 is *denunciation*, showing how the crying sins of Nineveh are receiving their fit punishment (vv. 1-7), comparing her ruin with that of No-Amon (8-10), mocking under various images the impotence in which she finds herself (11-18), and pronouncing that she has sinned against humanity past redemption (19).

With some brief observations on the features of Nahum's war-song this chapter must be concluded. In 2 1 the prophet descries the enemy —God's "hammer," as Assyria had once been His "axe" (Isa. 10 15)—and ironically rouses Nineveh to self-defence; comp. Jer. 51 12 (against Babylon). Vv. 3 and 4 disclose the besieging troops already in the environs; from 3*b* (comp. Ezek. 23 14. 15) it appears that "scarlet" was at this early period a fashionable military colour. As to ver. 5, "it is not easy to say whether" it "refers to besiegers or besieged" (A. B. Davidson): the latter reference is more plausible, these lines describing, perhaps with some errors in the text, the hurried and vain attempts made to strengthen and man the circuit of the walls.

From ver. 6 it appears that entrance is likely to be forced through the water-gates, where in fact Nineveh was most vulnerable. These gates were not situated on the river Tigris, which only touched the walls at one corner; probably they were the sluices regulating the flow of the Choser, a mountain stream entering the city from the east on its way to the river. This tributary was liable to floods, which might suddenly carry away its barriers and breach the adjoining walls. "Huzzab" in ver. 7 is quite obscure: from the sequel the word is taken to be an epithet used of the Assyrian *queen*, whose detection in the recesses of "the palace" (6) signalizes the enemy's complete possession of the city. The sense of ver. 8, again, is broken; it conveys the impression of a universal panic seizing the huge population, for centuries undisturbed by any foe; in the next verse we watch the ransacking of Nineveh's vast hoard of treasures. Happily the text of vv. 11, 12, developing the powerful figure of *the lion's den*, reads quite smoothly. In ver. 13 the triumph-ode reaches a pause; "Jehovah of hosts" reveals Himself, the Great Avenger behind the Median army which effects this prodigious ruin.

The revelation of God's hand in the tragedy leads to reflexion on its moral causes, the consideration of which chiefly occupies chap. 3.

Nineveh, in fact, has played throughout her career *the wild beast* among her neighbours (2 11-13)—alike in cruelty and cunning. Her eminence is in "lies and rapine"; she has "preyed unceasingly" on fellow nations (3 1). Her end is according to her works; she "falls by the sword," as she has lived by it. Vv. 2 and 3 contain the most vivid battle-picture in the whole poem:

Hark, the whip! and hark, the rattling of wheels!
And the galloping horse, and the dancing war-chariot!
    Horsemen at the charge!
And the flame of the sword, and gleam of the spear!

And a multitude of the slain, and a mass of carcases—no
    end to the corpses!
    And they stumble over the corpses.

The first three lines above describe the enemy's charge; the last two the carnage left in its track. Nineveh's "whoredoms," which form a prominent heading in her indictment (ver. 4), may signify the seductions of her commerce (see ver. 16; comp. Isa. 23 16ff., and pp. 74–75 above), with its dishonest practices and demoralizing influence on less civilized peoples; or may denote political intrigue and corruption, the systematic undermining of loyalty and independence in other nations by Assyria, of which Judæan history under Manasseh afforded an example; both modes of debasement may have been in Nahum's thoughts: the punishment is a harlot's disgrace, that of public stripping (5-7; comp. Isa. 3 17, Jer. 13 22-26, Ezek. 16 35-41).

"The rivers" of ver. 8, "amidst" which No-Amon is "situate," are the waters of the Nile with its canals (comp. Gen. 41 1, etc., Exod. 1 22, etc., Ezek. 29 3, etc.; where the same peculiar Hebrew term appears, appropriated to the Nile and its branches): this mighty river is called a "sea," as in Isa. 19 5. In the array of No-Amon's useless "helpers," "Put" (R.V.) is taken to signify a North African tribe (so probably in Gen. 10 6) connected with the "Lybians" (*Lubim* of the text); or it represents the "Punt" of Egyptian inscriptions, located by Egyptologists in modern Somali-land. Ver. 12 intimates that at the moment of writing Assyria's frontier fortresses are as yet standing; the war that is to prove so calamitous is beginning, and the prophet's imagination has outstripped the pace of history. There is no intrinsic difficulty and nothing contrary to the essential fulfilment of the prediction in supposing, as we have inclined to do, that Nahum prophesied at the earlier invasion of Assyria by the Medes about the year 630, although the final overthrow was postponed until the second invasion, which we now know took place above twenty years later. The estimate of Assyria's military power given in vv. 13-18 may well have been formed so soon as this by a keen observer, noting the signs of political collapse which ensued after Asshurbanipal's great struggle with Babylon and Elam (see pp. 179-180 above).

One would rely on this closing passage, rather than on the verses of military description, as evidence that the author had visited Nineveh. He appears to speak out of first-hand impressions, with the certainty and distinctness of personal observation, concerning its impending doom. He has witnessed the extinction of warlike spirit in the populace (ver. 13.), and the supine condition of the Assyrian nobility (17. 18); he foresees plainly and predicts triumphantly that the great tyrant city will fall to her assailants, past the hope of rising. The empire is sick at heart; Nineveh is morally effete and bankrupt.

ANALYSIS OF NAHUM'S POEM

The Double Title, Chap. 1 1.

I. THE INTRODUCTION: Chap. 1 2-10; 13. 15 2 2, 1 11. 12. 14 2 1.

    1. The Prelude, on *Jehovah the Avenger*, Chap. 1 2-10.
       (*a*) Jehovah's Character in Administration, 2. 3.
       (*b*) The Terribleness of His doings in Nature, 4 &c.

     (c) His Tenderness toward His afflicted People, 7.
     (d) His overwhelming Vengeance upon Evil Powers, 8-10.
  2. *Message of Deliverance to Judah*, Chap. 1 13. 15 2 2.
  3. *Message of Threatening to Assyria*, Chap. 1 11. 12 (see R.V. margin); 14 2 1.

II. THE SONG OF JEHOVAH'S TRIUMPH OVER NINEVEH : Chap. 2 3—3 19.

  1. *The Siege and Capture of the City*, Chap. 2 3-13.
     (a) The Besieging Forces in view, 3. 4.
     (b) The Summons to Defence, 5.
     (c) Breach at the Water-gates, 6.
     (d) Sack of the City ; its vast Wealth, 7-9.
     (e) The Empty Den of the Old Lion, 10-13.
  2. *Nineveh's Crimes and Punishment*, Chap. 3.
     (a) Deceit and Rapacity receive their Due, 1.
     (b) The Battle round the Walls, 2. 3.
     (c) A Harlot's Disgrace, 4-7.
     (d) The Fate of No-Amon rehearsed in Nineveh, 8-11.
     (e) Collapse of her Defences, 12-15.
     (f) Cowardice of her Traders, 16. 17.
     (g) Helplessness of her Nobles, 18.
     (h) Universal Applause at her Exit, 19.

So the Assyrian age ends, and with it a memorable chapter in the course of prophecy, and in the Divine dealings with Israel and the nations. Asshur was the first, as Rome was the last, in the procession of world-kingdoms that traverse the stage of revelation, to receive their doom one after another from Jehovah's mouth.

Amongst all the empires of the past, Asshur fell most miserably, and has been most completely effaced from human memory. In the year 400 B.C. Xenophon and his Greeks marched over the ruins of Nineveh quite unawares, and found them as they still remain. The catastrophe was a delayed but awful vindication of Jehovah's sovereignty over the peoples, and of the principles of justice preached by Isaiah and his companions in the eighth century. Later prophets point, tacitly, to this judgement, seeing in it a speaking evidence of the faithfulness of their God and the irresistible might lodged in His word. In this sense the Second Isaiah sets forth Jehovah as One who "bringeth princes to nothing," and "maketh the judges of the earth of none effect . . . Yea, He bloweth upon them, and they wither; and the whirlwind carrieth them away as stubble" (40 $_{23, 24}$). Musing on the fate of Nineveh and her sisters, the poet of Isaiah 25, still later, breaks out:

O Jehovah, Thou art my God;
I will exalt Thee, I will praise Thy name!
For Thou hast wrought wonders; Thy counsels of far-off times are faithfulness and truth.
For Thou hast made of a city a mound, of a fortress city a ruin-heap;
A palace of the aliens Thou hast made to be no city,— for ever it shall remain unbuilt!

PRINTED BY
HAZELL, WATSON AND VINEY, LD.,
LONDON AND AYLESBURY.

www.ingramcontent.com/pod-product-compliance
Lightning Source LLC
Chambersburg PA
CBHW020817230426
43666CB00007B/1042